You Mean
I Have
a Choice?

You Mean
I Have
a Choice?

Charles P. Lutz

AUGSBURG PUBLISHING HOUSE
MINNEAPOLIS, MINNESOTA

YOU MEAN I HAVE A CHOICE?

Library of Congress Catalog Card No. 78-158998

International Standard Book No. 0-8066-1131-6

MANUFACTURED IN THE UNITED STATES OF AMERICA

To
the woman
who lets me continue to choose her . . .
and keeps choosing me right back

Contents

Preface

"When you have to make a choice and don't make it, that is in itself a choice."—William James

Making choices is, for some of us, the most painful part of life. And that can be a lot of pain, since life is really made up of a continuous chain of choices.

There is a good deal of concentration on the idea of choice in the Christian tradition. The message of the gospel is that God chooses men, he chooses them for freedom, and that freedom requires them to choose. In Christianity, life is not all predetermined. It is influenced by the choices we make—or fail to make.

This book is about choosing. Its eight chapters group into three major sections: first, the understanding in the biblical tradition of God as the One who chooses himself a people (Chapters 1-3); then two chapters concerning the human process and foundation—theological as well as psychological—of our choosing; finally, Chapters 6-8 deal with some of the specific issues around which important choices are being made these days, by churches, by nations, by the human race.

Our method is to deal with the questions that face us in these areas—sometimes suggesting answers but always trying to get the question stated clearly and fairly. Here are samples of those questions:

- If God chose some, does that mean he chose not to choose others?

- How can we identify God's chosen people today? Is it the Christians? the Jews? the Americans? the prosperous?

- Does Christianity offer an ethical system to guide us in the choices we must make?

- Why are personal choices easy to make for some of us, but extremely troublesome for others?

- Why do churches often seem to use such bad process or style in making their institutional choices?

- Where did we Americans get the idea we were chosen to bring salvation to the world?

- Has our future come to a choice between money and trees, cars and clean beaches?

I will be arguing that we still do have meaningful choices, that it is you and I (not those others, or governments, or even God) who must make them, and that those choices make a difference. It is obvious that no choices are easy—or those that are we don't bother to write about. But Martin Luther had a brash and healthy bit of advice about the dilemma of decision-making.

Luther believed firmly that, whatever we do, there is some impurity of motive and some unrighteousness of action attached to it. We need to ask God to forgive not only our obvious failings but also our doing of good. We are simultaneously saints and sinners, and this dual status affects everything that we do.

Since we cannot choose *any* course of action which is absolutely free of sin, totally right, Luther concluded that we should "sin boldly." In other words, we make our choices with boldness, conscious that we live always in God's forgiveness.

John Morley, the 19th century English editor, is credited with saying that "in politics the choice is constantly between two evils." That's true not only in politics, but in all of life. So, our task is to find the best choice possible among the evil-containing options available—and then to "sin boldly!"

The chapters which follow offer a point of view—the author's. They do not pretend to contain all possible points of view. They certainly will not bring you an official point of view of any church body—although I hope and believe these thoughts are validly within the mainstream of classical Christian thinking. In the end, my ideas are offered as nothing more than springboards for your own thinking — or rethinking — about some important themes. That's all. That's plenty!

I want to thank all who contributed insights to what follows. Most of them did so unwittingly but are given credit in the text wherever the origin of material was known. Dr. Larry Balter, a neighbor and friend, was helpful in leading me to some of the research on psychological factors in decision-making.

And my wife deserves recognition, not only for typing most of the manuscript and giving it her criticism, but for accepting it over a several-month period as my excuse for not responding to her list of "tasks for husband in his free time."

"The Lord your God has chosen you to be a people for his own possession, out of all the peoples that are on the face of the earth" (Deut. 7:6 RSV).

" . . . but God's choice stands, and they are his friends for the sake of the patriarchs" (Rom. 11:28 NEB).

1.

How Odd of God
to Choose the Jews

It isn't men alone who make choices. Both the Old and the New Testament Scriptures are filled with talk of the choosing done by the Father-God. That choosing is seen to have cosmic consequences.

The Hebrew Scriptures, those writings Christians call "Old Testament," have as a central theme the belief that God chose himself a people. They were, in fact, *made* a people by God's act of choosing them. Their identity as a people came in the beginning solely from a conviction that God had chosen them "out of all the peoples that are on the face of the earth."

In this chapter we shall talk about God's people-choosing. Later, we will look at the way that one divine choice continued to evolve historically and in the present experience of believers.

The Choice Was God's

Everybody knows *whom* God chose. According to the Hebrew Scriptures, they were the people called Israelites, sons of Israel, who was called Jacob until he had that weird wrestling match all one night by the brook. The unknown opponent did leave a clue to his identity. He said, "Your name shall no more be called Jacob, but Israel, for you have striven with God. . . . "

I take this to be a graphic depiction of the reality which the Israelite people knew had made them a people: they were, by definition, totally engaged with God. More often opposed to him than with him, perhaps—but always engaged! To be a son of Israel meant just that, for "Israel" is "he who strives with God."

Israel, of course, was the son of Isaac, the one God *chose* to spare. Here too, through a cliff-hanging story, we learn of God's decision to save Isaac from the knife in his father's hand, a knife which, incredibly, God had caused to be there in the first place. Again, there was the reminder that the people of Israel lived by the grace of God's choice. Never mind that it sometimes seemed arbitrary or capricious. The point of the story was that God *chose* to save Isaac, so that a people might be born.

And Isaac was the son of Abraham, where God's choosing began. Abraham too went through a name change. From Abram to Abraham. From "exalted father" to "father of a multitude." The choosing of Abraham was expressed in the form of a covenant. It was given full form later with Moses. But the covenant really began back there with the choosing of Abraham: "Behold, my covenant is with you, and you shall be the father of a multitude of nations."

Ever after, through all their history, the Israelites not only identified themselves as the people chosen by God, but they identified God in terms of his choosing them. Who was their God? He was the one who chose Abraham. The prophet Nehemiah quotes Ezra: "Thou art the Lord, the God who didst choose Abram and bring him forth out of Ur of the Chaldeans and give him the name Abraham ... and didst make with him the covenant. . . . "

So these are the people God chose—those called Israelites in times past and their modern descendants, the Jews. The word "Jew" originally referred to those of the tribe of Judah, one of Jacob's sons; eventually Jew came to mean any of the Hebrew people. Later we will explore the relationship of the contemporary Jewish people to the covenant and the chosen-people question.

Right now, we need to consider some other questions concerning God's choice back then, as we hear about it through the Hebrew Scriptures: *how* did God choose Israel? *why* did he choose them and not some other group? and *for what purpose* did he choose them?

We have to say first that God chose Abraham and his children solely out of his sovereign will. He didn't consult with anyone, as far as we know. And the people of Israel certainly did not choose him. The initiative was all God's. The *how* of the choice was simply that one day God chose.

There's more to be said about the *why.*

It would be human to assume that the Israelites were

picked because they were superior in some way. They must have been better, more righteous, smarter than those not chosen. Well, listen to Moses:

"Do not say in your heart . . . , 'It is because of my righteousness that the Lord has brought me in to possess this land'; . . . Know therefore that the Lord your God is not giving you this good land to possess because of your righteousness; for you are a stubborn people" (Deut. 9:4, 6).

Then perhaps it was because the Israelites were a *large* people, more numerous than those skipped over. Moses had a word about that possibility too:

"It was not because you were more in number than any other people that the Lord set his love upon you and chose you, for you were the fewest of all peoples" (Deut. 7:7).

Again and again, the leaders and prophets of the Hebrews had to remind them that the reason for God's choice of Israel was to be found in God alone, not in them. The closest the prophets come to giving any kind of clue leaves it still in God's good pleasure:

"The Lord set his heart in love upon your fathers and chose their descendants after them" (Deut. 10:15).

Not only was God's choice of Israel unmerited by Israel, it was also irrational. There was no logical reason for it which could be reasoned out in the minds of men.

This sort of behavior on God's part is rather irritating to men, to put it mildly. To be picked out from among many, and to be told that you have been thus set apart— and then to be denied the fun of taking credit for being somehow special. That's a dirty trick!

The frustration is depicted well in Paddy Chayefsky's

delightful play *Gideon,* which had a successful run on Broadway in the early 1960s. God appears in the form of an angel or messenger to Gideon, a clumsy, donkey-like figure who is persuaded by God to go against 120,000 Midianites with a band of "300 uncompromising cowards," armed only with oil lamps and trumpets. God's purpose is to demonstrate that the protection of his people is not won by Gideon, but is given by God's grace. After the Midianites are routed in terror, Gideon and God (the angel) sit and talk. They discuss the persons with whom God has enjoyed face-to-face relationships and has come to appreciate with a special fondness. Then . . .

GIDEON: What is it that you love in me, my Lord? These other men were saints or prophets, but I am an ordinary sort. I am as all men are.

ANGEL: Well, perhaps *that* is your special attraction, your ordinariness. I would have plain men love me, not just saints.

GIDEON: Well, that isn't very nice.

ANGEL: Oh, Gideon, you are difficult.

GIDEON: Well, I do not think it gratifying to be loved for one's lack of distinction. *(He stands, ruffled.)* I thought I managed my duties well tonight.

ANGEL: Indeed you did.

GIDEON: To speak plainly, I think I made a good show of being a general. I have a commanding voice and am not unhandsome in my armor.

ANGEL: You make a splendid figure.

GIDEON: You find me amusing.

ANGEL: Well, you are a pompous ass.

GIDEON: I have had very little esteem in my life, my Lord, and I do not think there is much harm in my relishing this one moment of honor. I have this one son, Jether, who is 12 years old, the son of my first wife, and even he uses me lightly. . . .

ANGEL: I shall give you 70 sons, Gideon; they shall praise your name. You shall know the ardor of many wives.

GIDEON: I should like that.

ANGEL: Oh, Gideon, I shall bless you. I shall make your fields to prosper. I shall make your cattle fat. Your father shall kneel before you and embrace your knees. All Israel shall say: "Regard Gideon; he is the most blessed of men, for he is beloved of God." You seem displeased by all this good fortune.

GIDEON: Yes, well, all this greatness, all this good fortune which you will make mine, will not really be mine. It is all but a gift from God. There is no honor that reflects to *me* in it at all, merely that I am beloved of God.

ANGEL: Well, that is a somewhat less than gracious thing to say. The love of God will not suffice for you, indeed!

GIDEON: *(ashamed)* I spoke coarsely, Lord. Forgive me.[1]

Gideon's coarse speaking was also honest speaking. When God chooses a people, or a person, those chosen would like to think it was because God saw something special in them.

It is not so.

And therefore those who are chosen have no cause to be proud or to lord it over the unchosen. Israel had to be reminded again and again of this. When pressed for a reason behind his choosing, God is likely to say something like, "perhaps *that* is your special attraction, your ordinariness," Small comfort in that.

It's important to us men to know for what reasons we are chosen. We should also ask, to what *purpose* are we chosen? What end does God have in view when he chooses some from the many?

The Scriptures suggest a couple of possibilities concerning Israel. On the one hand, the choosing of Israel seems to be *an end in itself*. On the other, God seems to be choosing Israel to be the bearer of his good will and mercy to all men, *as a means to the end* of blessing the whole world.

Israel usually preferred to stress the former possibility, since to be a chosen people in that sense meant to enjoy the special favor of God and to be the recipient of special blessings from which the non-chosen were excluded.

The other possibility, that through a chosen people God would extend his love to all peoples, is not nearly so attractive. It not only implies that the special status is temporary. It also implies a burden—a mission or responsibility.

And the result could be a special sort of shame if one failed.

How often Israel wished for a return to the simple, ordinary status of being just another people, without any special expectations laid upon her!

Still, there was that element of honor in being the vessel through which God would bless all mankind, even if God wouldn't allow her to take any credit for being chosen. And that was the other thing special about Israel's chosenness: the special sort of frustration which resulted. Being chosen brought both a burden Israel didn't want and an honor she couldn't give up!

Are Today's Jews Still the Chosen People?

The second question we need to consider involves today's descendants of the Israelites. Are the modern Jews still a part of the historic chosen people? The question should be approached from two perspectives: what do the Jews themselves say about it, and what has been the attitude of non-Jews, particularly Christians?

Most current Jewish thought agrees that the Jews have had a special role to play in history—one could even say a unique role. And that uniqueness has been related to the Jewish people's historic sense of chosenness. Those who identify consciously as Jews today, whether or not they think of themselves as religious, invariably seem to have a sense of calling as they live out their existence in the world of non-Jews. *Because* they are Jews, a special responsibility is laid upon them.

There is a commitment to justice and peace, through

compassion for the persecuted and distressed. There remains the sense of being ordained in some special way as history's redemptive people. Undoubtedly, this often has led Jews to think of themselves as a *superior* people. Other peoples face the same temptation, but for the Jews it would be possible to root the sense of superiority in God's choice of them to play history's special role.

No way! A superiority complex has simply not been allowed by true Judaism. Listen to Rabbi Murray Saltzmann of the Indianapolis Hebrew Congregation:

> Judaism never entertained the idea that the Jew had a particular role in history because he possessed special innate endowments. The notion of racial superiority, expressed in whatever way, was repudiated at the very inception of Jewish history. . . . Human well-being, not Jewish well-being, was the goal of the covenant between Israel and God.[2]

Rabbi Saltzmann points to the Yiddish word *mentsh* as descriptive of the result when Judaism shaped the kind of human being God desired. A *mentsh* is an individual who is open to "becoming a loving, generous, intellectually developed, spiritually sensitized, and morally effective human being."

He adds that some observers today "see the crisis of Jewish survival as stemming from an overemphasis, on the part of some Jews, on current social issues such as civil rights or peace in Vietnam. They fear that these activities, because they may place the Jew in a vulnerable position of controversy, tend to arouse hatred of all Jews. But it is precisely this kind of involvement which Jewish tradition considers necessary in the development of *mentsh*. And the non-Jew's evaluation of the Jew must begin with this yardstick, not with race or genes."

The Jews' insistence on maintaining a distinct identity, despite all that the non-Jewish world could dream up to destroy it, comes basically from their understanding of chosenness. God made a covenant with *them*. That covenant still stands.

It's true that being chosen has brought the Jews suffering more than success or power. That's the way God said it would be.

How have non-Jews, especially Christians whose roots are in that same covenant, viewed the continuing Jewish claim to being a uniquely chosen people? There are three broad types of response to the question:

Some Christians have said, "The Jews aren't God's chosen people any more, unless they have accepted Jesus Christ." This position has held that with the rejection of Jesus the Jews gave up their claim to being the chosen ones. The "spiritual Israel" since Christ is Christianity, in this view.

As Jews see it, this is asking them to stop being Jews in order to become "the new Israel." It's no wonder very few Jews have accepted the offer through the past 19 centuries. Especially when you realize that the people they were being invited to join had certain behavior patterns which looked inferior to the Jews, to say the least!

Even Martin Luther, who often had harsh words for the Jews, once confessed: "If the Apostles . . . had behaved toward us Gentiles as we Gentiles behave toward the Jews, not one Gentile would have become a Christian." [3]

Despite that admission of failure, however, Luther continued to think that Jews would be happier, more blessed, more complete if they could know Christ as Messiah. It should not be surprising that Christians would hold such a view. After all, anyone who has found a good thing will want to share it, unless he is totally selfish.

A second kind of response has been less common. It is the argument that the Jews must be *the* chosen people for all time because they are clearly history's superior people. The British writer C. P. Snow gave new impetus to this viewpoint a few years ago in a much-publicized speech at a Jewish seminary in Cincinnati.

Snow, who is not a Jew, argued that the Jews possess a genetic pool which is superior to that of non-Jews. Only this could account for what he saw to be the extraordinary intelligence, moral consciousness, and drive which make Jews leaders in many fields of human endeavor.

It may well be that centuries of suffering *have* shaped a special sort of people—unusually gifted, sensitive and tough because only such survived. But this is a debate without possibility of resolution. Let me simply repeat: the Scriptures and modern Judaism alike insist that Israel was *not* chosen because of superior morality, intellectuality, ability, or even humility.

The final viewpoint is the one I favor. It is that the Jews remain God's chosen people. But they are not his *only* chosen people.

One Covenant—Two Approaches?

It may be that God has two ways of coming to mankind. One way is through his ancient covenant with Israel. The other way, through Christ, is God's way of extending *that same covenant* to include all nations. Christianity is then the Jewish covenant taken to the non-Jewish world. In a way, the very rejection by the Jews of that Jew, Jesus, opened the possibility for the Gentiles to get in on the kind of relationship with God that the Jews were always privileged to have.

St. Paul sees Judaism and Christianity as fellow heirs of God's grace. Can God have two approaches, one for the Jews and one for the Gentiles? Biblically, there are difficulties with this interpretation, just as there are with the understanding that Jews can be God's people today *only* by renouncing Judaism and accepting a Christian belief in Jesus. Certainly Christians who have found that Jesus is the central meaning in their lives will continue to express that meaning to those within reach, including Jews—it would be dishonest not to do so. But having said that, I still believe St. Paul had something of a dual-covenant idea in mind when he wrote these words:

" . . . this partial blindness has come upon Israel only until the Gentiles have been admitted in full strength; when that has happened, the whole of Israel will be saved. . . . In the spreading of the Gospel they are treated as God's enemies for your sake; but God's choice stands, and they are his friends for the sake of the patriarchs. . . . Just as formerly you were disobedient to God, but now have received mercy in the time of their disobedience, so now, when you receive mercy, they have proved disobedient, but only in order that they too may receive mercy. For . . . God's purpose was to show mercy to all mankind" (Rom. 11:25-32, NEB).

God's choice stands!

Did we in our own strength confide
Our striving would be losing;
Were not the right Man on our side,
The Man of God's own choosing.

—Martin Luther

2.

The Man of God's Own Choosing

If Christians find it odd that God should choose the Jews, they consider it ironic that the Jews should un-choose the One God chose from their midst.

As Christians see it, God chose Israel to be the people who would bring forth Messiah (the Anointed One). When it happened in Jesus, his own people did not honor him.

Well, the Jews are still God's friends, according to St. Paul, "for the sake of the patriarchs." For the rest of us, Christ appears to be God's clearest way of making known his purpose. Again, we're told, it was a matter of choice, God's choice.

In this chapter we shall explore two main ideas. One is that Jesus is significant precisely *because* God chose him. The second is that Jesus, once chosen by the Father, did some choosing of his own.

The One Chosen by God

Christianity in the past several centuries has pushed harder on the divinity of Jesus than on his humanity. Both emphases are biblical. Jesus is fully God and fully a human being, as the New Testament sees him. To man's rationality, that's impossible. Still, to talk about Jesus as exclusively divine or exclusively human is clearly not a biblical way. We do our best to grasp this mystery. But we always stress one of the two natures more than the other.

It seems to me that what the world needs now is Jesus the Man, the true Human Being, the only complete human being who has lived. So let's talk about Jesus, the "Man of God's own choosing."

There is an old heresy. It was given the label "adoptionism." As early as the second century after Christ there were people who taught that Jesus at his birth was no more than a man like any other. God adopted him as his Son, they taught, by giving him miraculous power, but he was not Son of God from the beginning. Some believed that Jesus' adoption came at his Baptism. Others felt he gradually acquired a divine nature which eventually earned him the designation "God." More recently, people have taught that Jesus was adopted as God's Son at the time of his resurrection.

We do not understand Christ to be God's chosen one in the adoptionist sense. The Christian faith has always insisted that Christ, from the beginning of his earthly life, was fully God and fully man. He was not just a man whom

God at some point decided to enter in a special way, or a man who gradually grew into full divinity.

And yet, the New Testament *does* talk about Jesus as the chosen one of God. When Jesus was up in the hills with Peter, John, and James, during what we call the Transfiguration, the disciples heard a voice, as from a cloud:

"This is my Son, my Chosen; listen to him!" (Luke 9:35).

Later, when Jesus was dying, Luke describes the rulers of the people as scoffing at the foot of the cross:

"He saved others; let him save himself, if he is the Christ of God, his Chosen One" (Luke 23:35).

"Messiah" is the word for the one God would raise up to redeem his people Israel. Many in Jesus' day expected Messiah to be the one who would restore the Kingdom of Israel to its old glory. The disciples asked him about it and Jesus did not disown the term. But neither did he indicate very clearly in what sense he was Messiah. Some Bible students believe Jesus was not happy with the title because it had nationalistic associations he did not wish to encourage.

Still, it was clearly common knowledge that Jesus' followers saw him as, in some sense, the Chosen One. Thus the term is thrown at him by scoffers around the cross. Though there is little use of the term "Messiah" in the New Testament, the concept stayed alive—that Jesus was the one chosen by God to save his people. The Bible indicates that Jesus was chosen for this role from the foundation of the world, before history began, in the eternal plan of the Father. His disciples, however, did not perceive his Messianic role in any meaningful way until after his death and resurrection.

Karl Barth, the great 20th century theologian, writes that Jesus is significant because it is through him that God chose to reveal himself. And what he reveals preeminently, says Barth, is that God chooses to be for and with every man unconditionally. In the election of Jesus, Barth believes, God commits himself to the election (choosing) of every man.

Christianity has always seen the meaning of history coming to its most intense focus in Jesus. Earlier, God had chosen himself a people. Now, from that people, he chooses a Person. The consequence is a broadening of the covenant, of God's wish to be with men. Through Jesus, a Jew, the God-man covenant goes to non-Jews as well. He is the firstfruits of a new people. Jesus, the Chosen One, responds to God on behalf of the world of human beings, of whom he is one.

"He is the first-born of many brothers, not only in resurrection but in rendering obedience to God. His obedience was a sort of pioneering and representative obedience; he obeyed on behalf of men. . . . " [1]

Jesus represents me, you, all mankind in living his life of perfect obedience, even to death. As with the people from whom he comes, he demonstrates that to be chosen is to suffer. And suffering, in some form or other, is what it means to live a life wholly for others.

Because Jesus goes on ahead as a pioneer, many are able to follow in his path. And the writer of First Peter is able to apply the special language of the original covenant people to those who now come after Christ, the chosen:

"You are a chosen race, a royal priesthood, a holy nation, God's own people . . . " (1 Peter 2:9).

The Chosen One Chooses

The building up from the one Person to the countless throngs of the new covenant people begins when Jesus does some choosing of his own.

First, he chooses the twelve. Why that number? Undoubtedly to suggest the completeness of Israel, which is made up of twelve tribes.

It is clear from the Gospel accounts that *he* chose *them,* not the other way around. In fact, it appears that most of them had shown little inclination to become followers until he chose them. At one point, Jesus reminded them pointedly that he had done the choosing, not they, and that his choosing had included the one who would betray him. "Did I not choose you, the twelve, and one of you is a devil?" (John 6:70).

The twelve were not allowed to select themselves for membership in that small band, but presumably they were free to refuse. It is not recorded that any who were invited did refuse. But the freedom was there for Judas later to choose the route of betrayal. Peter chose a similar route at one point, then turned back in remorse and was restored to the group.

It would be worthwhile taking a quick look again at the kinds of men Jesus chose. In some cases we know a good deal about these men, in others very little. They were a diverse lot:

Simon Peter, who had a talent for confronting and being confronted

James, son of Zebedee, the quiet one of the inner three

John, his brother, who had the gift of intimacy

Andrew, who was first to say "We have found the Messiah"

Philip, who asked to be shown the Father and was pointed to Jesus

Nathanael (or Bartholomew), who wondered what good could come out of Nazareth

Matthew, tax-collector and collaborator, perhaps the most unlikely choice

Thomas, a twin, who was sometimes perplexed

James, son of Alphaeus, prototype of all the silent disciples through the ages

Thaddaeus (the other Judas), who wondered how Jesus would be revealed to the world

Simon the Zealot, of the Jewish underground

Judas Iscariot, who demonstrated that not even God can force a man to love him

The question most bewildering to all subsequent disciples through the centuries had been: why did Jesus choose these particular 12? Was it more than chance? Did he foresee in them certain qualities he wanted in his core of initial followers? If so, how did the betrayer come to be included? Or did each of the 12 have the traitor's potential?

Further, why does the Bible say that few are chosen, when it also says that God is "the Savior of all men"? Does God choose some to salvation and others to damnation, as certain Christians have taught?

Questions like these, and the incomprehensible interplay between man's freedom and God's, we'll explore in the next chapter.

"You did not choose me, but I chose you and appointed you that you should go and bear fruit" (John 15:16).

3.

But Few Are Chosen

Now we come to the tough part. What do we do with the Bible's teachings that (1) God wants all men to be in relationship to him, and (2) God *chooses* some but not all for fellowship with himself? Two summary sentences of Scripture, which illustrate the seeming conflict, are these:

> "God our Savior . . . desires all men to be saved and to come to the knowledge of the truth" (1 Tim. 2:3-4).
> "For many are called but few are chosen" (Matt. 22:14).

We grapple here with the Christian doctrine of election, which has often troubled the community of the faithful. It is clear from the Scriptures that God desires reconciliation with all of his creatures. It is also evident that for God's will to triumph in the lives of all men the human freedom of some would need to be violated.

The Classical Doctrine of Election

Both emphases are in the Bible: first that Christ will draw *all* men to him and in him "shall *all* be made alive"; second that God calls many but chooses few. The main strain of Christian thought, however, has usually been on the side of the latter, a position of particularism or of anti-universalism.

The doctrine of election has said that God indeed chooses some, out of the many who are called, for salvation in the name of Jesus Christ. However, what would seem to be a logical corollary, that God also chooses some for damnation, has *not* been a part of the classical teaching of election.

In other words, election is not to be equated with predestination. Predestination is the view that from the beginning God ordained that certain human beings should be inside and others outside his fellowship. A rigid form of Calvinism (sometimes called "double predestination"), taught that God elected every individual *either* to the company of the saved *or* to the company of the damned, and that he did his choosing before the foundation of the world. Most Christians have rejected such a cold extension of human logic.

Other Christians have tried to explain election in terms of God's foreknowledge. For example, in view of the faith in Christ which he foresaw certain individuals would have, God "elected" them to eternal salvation. But this has its weakness also, since it suggests that God's choice is conditioned by the response of man, known in advance.

Difficult as it is, the Scriptural teaching is that the choice remains entirely with God. Just as the initiative was all in

God with the choosing of Abraham and the Israelite nation, so it is for the believer in Christ.

The one who is a part of the redeemed must therefore give all the credit to God's grace. But the one who is excluded has only himself to blame. This is the only way to put it, since it is the only way to account for the element of *freedom*.

God has a certain freedom: the freedom to seek his will among his creatures.

Man also has a freedom: the freedom to say no to God.

If both God and man have a measure of true freedom, the freedom of neither is absolute. Both freedoms are relative. Man's because he is man, a limited finite being. God's because he respects the dignity of his creation, including the right of the creature to reject him.

Norman H. Snaith comments on this paradox in *A Theological Word Book of the Bible,* describing the biblical significance of the word "choose." When one first understands that he has been redeemed, Snaith writes,

> a man is very sensible of the fact that he has a choice between Christ and not-Christ, between life and death. . . .
>
> But afterwards that same man grows more and more conscious that even those very first stirrings in his own heart which led him to choose Christ were the work of the Holy Spirit. He becomes growingly sure that he was chosen, rather than that he chose. . . . Further, this same man is not prepared to follow the logic of this statement along normal human lines to its conclusion, for then he will find himself saying that God has not chosen certain others, from which it is

> but a small step to say that he has elected some to
> damnation. . . . We say, therefore, that the idea of a
> human choice is the language of the newly converted,
> but that the certainty of the divine choice is the lan-
> guage of the sanctified.[1]

This understanding of election, and the anti-universalism
it implies, underscores God's respect for man's free will.
Even if some spurn him forever, God will not force them
to love him.

My favorite expression of this concept is in C. S. Lewis'
The Great Divorce, that witty and wise discussion of Heav-
en and Hell. In discussing why some folks go one way,
some the other, Lewis has The Teacher say:

> There are only two kinds of people in the end:
> those who say to God, "Thy will be done," and those
> to whom God says, in the end, *"Thy* will be done."
> All that are in Hell choose it. Without that self-choice,
> there would be no Hell.[2]

Those who insist on their own way are permitted to
choose it, eternally. Thus even eternal separation from God
is an ironic witness to God's respect for the freedom he
built into his creature man, a freedom he will not violate.

That, at least, is how I understand the classic Christian
doctrine of election. But there is another way of looking
at the whole question.

The Case for Universalism

We can speak properly about God having redeemed *the
entire world* in Christ. It is a world for which Christ gave

his life, *all of it,* and which in his resurrection is made new, *all of it.*

And I mean not only all of humankind, but the rest of creation as well. " . . . the creation itself will be set free from its bondage to decay and obtain the glorious liberty of the children of God. We know that the whole creation has been groaning in travail together until now" (Rom. 8:21-22). In Colossians 1, Christ is presented as the reconciler of *all things,* on earth and in heaven.

The point is that, in the world of men and of nature, there is already at work a process of reconciliation. This may not be known to the world, at least not to all of it. But it is reality, according to the Scriptures.

It is true that many do not know what God has done and is doing in his world. They may be those who have chosen to remain separate from the new life. They may be those who have heard nothing about it.

In any case, they are within the healing work of God in Christ. Jesus no doubt had them in mind when he spoke about "other sheep of mine, not belonging to this fold, whom I must bring in" (John 10:16). The writer of 1 Timothy (4:10) speaks of God as "the Savior of all men, especially of those who believe." He does *not* say "only of those who believe"!

The sole difference then between Christians and others is that Christians *know* what has happened to the world because of Christ. This knowledge gives them no special privileges. They cannot pull rank on other men. Their only real distinction is that they have been let in on the secret

—and are expected to share it. They have been given the message of reconciliation.

Those who have the message are normally in the fellowship of the church. Or, we define "church" as those who have committed themselves to the reality of that message. But we are not loved of God *because* we are church members. It is the other way around. Because we are loved of God, and have come to know it, we identify with others who have had the same experience, and we call this fellowship the church.

Let's be very clear: we have received God's love because we are a part of the entire *world* he loves. How ridiculous then for Christians to talk as though Jesus is their private possession. As Harold Ditmanson, professor of religion at St. Olaf College, once wrote in a paper on the doctrine of grace:

> A Christian witness is not trying to change people so much as he is trying to make them aware of what they really are in the new relationship. . . . The point is not that the Christian has something other men do not have, but that all men have something that too many men do not know they have and as a result are suffering just as if they did not have it.

It may be asked: if this is a correct understanding of what has happened, why should we bother to preach the gospel? If redemption has already come to the whole world, what's the point of doing evangelistic work so that more men may know about it?

The point is exactly the same as the point of telling a

convict that he has been pardoned by the governor. The pardon may come through at a certain hour, and be known to the governor and his staff, to the warden, the press, possibly to the whole state or nation. It is a legal fact that the man has been pardoned and is therefore declared free.

But it is not a fact for the imprisoned man until it has been communicated to him and assimilated by him. He is not free until he receives the good news that he is free, and until the lock is turned and he sees that he may go through the gate. He is then able to enjoy the new life which has been granted.

This is why Christians tell others that they too have been freed: it is only when you know about it that you may live as a liberated person. That living is not a simple thing. It takes a lifetime of working at it, practicing the reconciliation which God has already given. It is a reconciliation with at least four dimensions: between myself and God, among my various selves, between myself and the non-human creation, and between myself and other persons. It is the latter which seems to cause us the most difficulty today—maybe in every age.

The Bible is clear that when the gospel comes to any group of persons, it ends all distinctions. It does not eliminate them, but they are no longer of ultimate consequence. They are not justification for separation, or enmity, or class rankings. The gospel abhors polarizations among men and works toward breaking down all of them.

Christ has created "a single new humanity in himself, thereby making peace" (Eph. 2:15 NEB). There can be no separation of Jew and Gentile, male or female, slave and free man—in the light of the gospel's reconciliation. We can add to the list from our current categories of polarization among North Americans:

> black and white
> young and old
> poor and rich
> women and men
> educated and less educated
> capitalist and socialist
> intellectual elite and Middle American majority

All of these polarizations, which may seem so deep and permanent, are declared to have no lasting significance because of God's activity in Christ.

The Gospel and Exclusivism

And we need to add one more to the list: the distinction between Christian and non-Christian. Even this separation has no ultimate standing, if we believe that *all* men have been made free, that the *whole* world has been redeemed. As the Study Document of the Helsinki Assembly of Lutheran World Federation (1963) says: "Jesus Christ is the act of God in which God has created salvation for all men."

We may speak legitimately of the distinction between Christian and non-Christian only in the terms used earlier. The Christian is not a better or wiser or more favored human being than the non-Christian. The Christian is simply one who, through no credit to himself, has been privileged to receive some knowledge about what God is up to in his world. The only thing which sets Christians apart is that they have been given the message of reconciliation and have been called to share it, by the way they live and the words they speak.

Where does this leave the whole business of *choice*—both God's and man's? We return to the earlier summary. God *chooses* to be reconciled to all. But because of the freedom God gave his creatures, a man may *choose* to go his own non-reconciled way. God has chosen the whole world in Christ, but the gift of new life in Christ is not forced on anyone.

Christianity has always had difficulty accepting this truth. Gregory Baum wrote about the problem in the July-August 1968 issue of *The Ecumenist*:

> The Christian religion divided mankind into we and they. This radical distinction influenced the way Christians understood their life in society, their personal associations as well as their political ideals. . . . We hold the truth; they are in error. We have access to salvation; they sit in darkness and are filled with fear. We are virtuous, understanding, liberated, cultured; they are treacherous, fanatical, superstitious, uncouth. . . . We are superior; they are inferior. . . . Christian literature is filled with such a rhetoric of exclusion. . . . It is this rhetoric of exclusion that has made Christianity a source of prejudice.
>
> The Gospel corrects the radical distinction between "we" and "they." The Gospel, moreover, rejects the radical distinction between "the holy" and the "unholy." Jesus has abolished the division between just and sinners. According to his teaching all men are sinners. . . .

The universality of which we speak is not undifferentiated human community. It is not envisaged as the removal of all distinctions. On the contrary, the particularity of one's own group must become the key for the appreciation and understanding of what particularity means and the bridge to the kind of pluralistic universality that we seek. In other words, it is not by becoming less Christian—or less faithful to another religion, I suppose—that a man loses his prejudices and experiences fellowship with others. On the contrary, it is by becoming more Christian . . . that a man is able to acknowledge other people for what they are and become willing to embrace them as brothers, without wishing to destroy their heritage and draw them into an undifferentiated religious melting pot.[3]

Human beings have always had a we/they mentality. There is something in us that wants to sort out people along in-group and out-group lines. We like to exclude, usually in order to make ourselves feel more important. But the gospel won't let us, not when the motivation is to bring special privilege to me and mine.

The gospel proclaims our common humanity, distressing as that may be to those who shudder at talk about "one world." We need somehow to hold this teaching always in tension with the doctrine of election.

"I offer you the choice of life or death, blessing or curse. Choose life and then you and your descendants will live"

(Deut. 30:19 NEB).

4.

Chosen . . . for Choosing

The Christian affirms that God has already made the ultimate choice. He has decided, once and for all, to throw in his lot with us. He has determined that the world of humankind is worth caring about.

But that's not the end of it. The fearsome wonder of God's choosing us is the responsibility it brings. We become a part of the unfolding of God's choice. We live in the warmth of his gracious acceptance. And we are expected, once chosen, to make choices.

All persons make choices, of course. What is different for those who know they are chosen is an over-all sense of direction. For the believer, there is but one basic choice. To the degree that his life is integrated, whole, consistent, all his choices will make sense in relation to that one ultimate choice.

One Basic Choice for Believers

It is not, as so many falsely believe, the choice between good and evil. It is rather the choice between death and life,

47

between despair and faith in resurrection, between separation and reconciliation.

The Deuteronomy passage at the head of this chapter speaks about our basic choice. We are to choose *life*. But having said that really doesn't help very much. The challenge is to discern what really is life-giving and what is not.

In Christ, we see that choosing life means choosing to be fully human. And *that* means choosing to live—and die—for others.

Sound strange? That the choice of life should mean, in the end, choosing to die for others? That's what the gospel is about. Dietrich Bonhoeffer, German Lutheran theologian who was imprisoned and then executed under Hitler, said that "when God calls a man he bids him come and die."

One definition of dying is the spending of one's life. This is what we're talking about. The one chosen by God is called to spend his life for others—and thus he chooses life.

Martin Luther King knew what this meant. He did not ask God for a long life, but for one that counted. He chose life by choosing to spend his, to use it up, in pursuit of a dream. He seemed to be aware that investing his life as he did could well mean an early end to it. The night before he was killed, he expressed that awareness clearly as he spoke to the Memphis garbage strikers.

> Like anybody, I would like to live a long life. Longevity has its place. But I'm not concerned about that now. I just want to do God's will. And he's allowed me to go up to the mountain. And I've looked over, and I've seen the promised land. I may not get there with you, but I want you to know tonight that we as

a people will get to the promised land. So I'm happy tonight. I'm not worried about anything. I'm not fearing any man.

Dr. King knew, as did Dietrich Bonhoeffer, that the final and root choice is the willingness to risk death. We are not chosen in order to hold onto life as something to be sheltered, but are chosen to spend it, use it, on behalf of others.

There is a somewhat different sense in which we choose life by facing the fact of our death. There is something profoundly liberating about my recognizing, emotionally as well as intellectually, that I won't get out of this life alive. Only by accepting the fact of my death, can I really live, as the gospel says: "Whoever seeks to gain his life will lose it, but whoever loses his life will preserve it" (Luke 17:33).

Death for the Christian represents the passage to resurrection, to eternal life. Even non-believers have seen this hope as the heart of the Christian faith. The contemporary German Marxist philosopher, Ernst Bloch, has written:

"It was not the morality of the Sermon on the Mount which enabled Christianity to conquer Roman paganism, but the belief that Jesus had been raised from the dead. In an age when Roman senators vied to see who could get the most blood of a steer on their togas—thinking this would prevent death—Christianity was in competition for eternal life, not for morality." [1]

So the Christian chooses life. But not by spurning death. It is through a kind of death, a spending, a giving away, a dying of self, that he lives his present life. It is through literal, physical death that he enters the life that is eternal.

Authentic freedom now is to be free enough to live for others. Ultimate and total freedom is in the promise that in dying we shall live. As the spiritual says: "Thank God almighty, I'm free at last!"

God's choice of me makes such a life of freedom, both now and after death, available. I live out that life by making my countless choices, large and small, alone and with others—in the confidence that God in his choosing of me knew what he was doing.

This is what I meant by that over-all sense of direction which can make all the difference to believers who make decisions. We know that God has made the ultimate decision for the healing of his world.

A Variety of Ethical Approaches

But there is more we can say about the basis for our own decision-making. The study of Christian ethics reveals a variety of ways in which Christians have sought to construct guidelines for their decision-making. An ethic is a systematic approach to pursuing that which is the good life, or, as a Christian might put it, to the doing of God's will.

In the remainder of this chapter, we shall look at some of the classical approaches to ethics which Christians have adopted. Dr. Hans-Ruedi Weber of the Ecumenical Institute in Switzerland (in a paper written for a lay course there) suggests that there are three chief types: (1) ethics of norms, (2) ethics of inspiration, and (3) ethics of middle axioms.

Ethics of norms are based on the assumption that there

are valid guidelines which are external and objective, essentially the same for everyone who accepts their validity.

One such ethical system is that which is based on natural law. The norm is whatever is faithful to human nature. The good is that which human beings consider as natural. Traditional Roman Catholic moral theology was based on a natural law approach. Behind that church's teaching against the so-called artificial methods of conception control, for example, has been the conviction that such methods interfere with the natural and are therefore immoral.

But, as the world's population problem is showing us, a natural law ethic can become static and more of a hindrance than a help to responsible decision-making. Studies of various human cultures suggest that there is no single human nature and that human nature can change. Efforts to reshape the ethics of natural law in a more dynamic way, recognizing the changeable character of human nature and of the human situation, are now under way.

Another ethic of norms is the type which is based on certain biblical texts or themes.

The difficulty with relying wholly on the Bible for a norm is that there is no single norm there, but a pluralism of norms. Biblical studies today are reminding us that the Scriptures contain a variety of theologies, a variety of emphases—and in different situations, various moral guidelines.

The Bible is preeminently useful to the Christian as a foundation for his ethical decision-making. But it is not very helpful as a codebook. It doesn't give you a good-for-all-time answer to questions like how many children should I have? may a person have more than one mate? is it all right to hold slaves?

Many Bible students today believe that the most appropriate use of the Scriptures is to apply to modern situations the broad biblical themes about God's love for man and man's responsibility for his neighbor. This leads to an ethic of the second type.

Ethics of inspiration assume a more internal and subjective foundation. One example with a sizeable following in recent years is situation ethics, in which the only criterion for an act is faithfulness to the love revealed in Jesus Christ. The good here is that which best fulfills the imperative to show love to the other in the present situation.

This kind of ethic also has its limitation. We are not helped with the question: love to whom? As. Dr. Weber says, "In looking after the good of an individual one may perpetuate a social evil. In changing evil social structures one must almost inevitably harm individuals."

It is also likely that in emphasizing the present situation we tend to forget where the situation came from (tradition) and where it will take us in the future (forecast). Dr. Weber suggests that situation ethics will be giving more attention to how we shape the future through our decision-making.

A second example of an ethic of inspiration is that which stems from a conscious living in the presence of God. The good is what comes from prayer and meditation, with emphasis on the reflection of Christ's image in us.

The usual weakness of this kind of ethic has been its individualism. The most pious people may not be able to show love to neighbor in social, economic, and political realms. We need to develop a spirituality which can help people in a complex and fast-changing world to show God's love not only in interpersonal but also in intergroup relations.

Ethics of middle axioms stand somewhere between the two other types. "Middle axioms," says Dr. Weber, "are those goals for society which are more specific than universal Christian principles and less specific than concrete institutions or programs of action."

One axiom which has influenced much Christian thought in recent decades is that our goal on earth is to work toward creation of "the responsible society." The good is that which brings the human condition closer to the situation described.

Most of the talk about "responsible society," however, has come from the North Atlantic Christians. Our brethren in the developing nations of the southern hemisphere are more likely to have liberation at the front of their thinking, and some of them have spoken of the need for an axiom about "the responsible revolution."

It is clear that middle axioms cannot be universal or unchanging. It should also be clear that none of the types of ethic we have considered is a totally satisfying guide to decision-making.

I suppose most of us, without realizing it, rely on a combination of ethical approaches. And that's fine. The important thing, I believe, is that we stop and reflect from time to time on the basis for our decisions.

The vast majority of our decisions are made without

reflection, spontaneously. And it has to be that way, or we'd never get through a day without great anguish. But occasionally we need to run a check on the habits, presuppositions, prejudices—the ethic—which underlie our decision-making. Dr. Weber argues that this is as necessary as the periodic physical check-up.

We Know Whose Side We're On

The important thing for Christians to know, whatever ethic or combination of ethical systems we choose to follow, is that we belong to a tradition which has always taken the side of the poor and the weak. That is, it has done so when faithful to itself.

From the background of the Ten Commandments to the Book of Job to the prophetic writings to the New Testament, righteousness is identified with seeing that the forgotten, the downtrodden, the underdog, the alienated, the unwanted, the powerless are treated well.

Mary reflects this theme in her Magnificat, recorded in Luke 1:

> My soul magnifies the Lord . . .
> He has scattered the proud in the imagination of their
>   hearts,
> He has put down the mighty from their thrones,
> And exalted those of low degree;
> He has filled the hungry with good things,
> And the rich he has sent empty away . . .

Jesus draws a similar focus when he chooses to read in the synagogue these words from the prophet Isaiah:

The Spirit of the Lord is upon me
Because he has anointed me to preach good news to
  the poor.
He has sent me to proclaim release to the captives
And recovering of sight to the blind
To set at liberty those who are oppressed . . .

(Luke 4:18)

The poor and the weak must be of special concern to the people of God because they are of special concern to God. If you want a guideline for the decisions Christians must make regarding their relationship to others, this is one that's basic.

In addition to ethical-theological factors, there are psychological ones involved in our making of choices. The next chapter begins with a brief look at the psychology of decision-making.

I have often thought morality may perhaps consist solely in the courage of making a choice.—Leon Blum.

Making decisions is easier for stupid people than for the intelligent.—Vladimir Zhemchuzhnikov.

5.

Our Choices Are Changing

Presidents of the United States like to talk about the loneliness of the decision-making responsibility that is theirs. I'm certain it must be so. The sense of being alone is surely intensified when the results of a choice have great consequence for perhaps billions of human beings.

But I want to argue that *every* choice made by an individual is finally his alone, no matter how much helpful counsel he may receive, and he must take responsibility for its results. The only difference between you or me and the President, then, is that he is in a position to affect many more people, perhaps all now living, with a single decision. Yours and mine, chances are, will not influence so many. But our choices can be just as lonely.

We will say something about individual choices in this chapter. There are things to be said about the difficulty of making choices, to begin with. Then we will take a brief look at three of the major life choices facing all of us.

Why Choices Are Hard to Make

Choosing is difficult for most human beings. But the process really hasn't been studied very much. We do know that all decision-making is easier for some persons than for others. We also know that certain kinds of decisions are easy for some personality types but hard for other types, and vice versa.

For example, it simply seems obvious that "making decisions is easier for stupid people than for the intelligent," as the Russian writer Zhemchuzhnikov said. Intelligent persons, we should expect, will weigh the possibilities more carefully and completely. They will have more information to feed into the choosing process. They are better able to project, to anticipate, to reflect about the deferred pains and joys. Therefore, intelligent people often find it difficult to make certain kinds of decision.

But there is another possibility. Some of us simply resist making decisions out of a profound fear of looking bad. And the longer we think about a decision which must be made, the greater becomes our panic about having to decide. Of course, not to choose is itself a choice. But we can deceive ourselves into thinking it is not.

One psychological study has concluded that there are just two broad categories of human being, when it comes to decision-making. The first are those in whom the motivation to achieve success is stronger than the motivation to avoid failure. The second are those in whom the motivation to avoid failure is stronger than the motivation to achieve success.

We are all made up of a mixture of both motivations, to be sure, but one must surely dominate the other most of the time. Those in the first category will be likely to make more risky choices. They will take chances, flirting with failure because of the promise of a success which is valued highly. Those in the second category will be more inclined to play it safe, since goofing up is to be avoided at all costs.

Without a doubt the world needs both kinds. For different tasks, different types are needed. In a bridge partner, I would prefer Type One, since my theory of bridge playing is that the reasonable risk-taker will usually come out ahead of the somewhat more cautious. But in a surgeon who is about to cut into me, I would probably prefer Type Two. It occurs to me that therein may lie the explanation for the extreme conservatism, *in non-medical matters,* of so many physicians. They tend to be cautious types, because the nature of their work compels them to be. The conservatism which properly belongs to the practice of medicine quite easily slips over into political and social areas.

For those of us who have great pain in choosing, there is some old advice attributed to Pythagoras. He supposedly said: "Choose always the way that seems the best, however rough it may be; custom will soon render it easy and agreeable."

The Range of Choices Keeps Growing

In addition to psychological factors, there is another reason why making choices seems to be getting more difficult. It really *is* more difficult in many areas of life because

of a rapid growth in the variety of options facing the one
who must choose.

First of all, we can think of the changes in the *quality*
of our choices. By quality I don't mean the wisdom or
morality of them, but the richness of options available
today, compared to yesterday. The easiest way to paint the
contrast is to mention the shift from rural to urban in
American social pattern.

Many observers of urbanization have pointed out that
the distinction between the rural and urban forms of existence is seen most sharply in the range of choices open to
an individual.

For example, in small-town Iowa as a boy I had only
one choice where motion pictures were involved—to go or
not to go. Until I left home for college, I never lived in a
town which had more than one movie theatre. So if I went
to the movies, I didn't choose a picture; I saw what was
showing. Today, in the metropolitan areas where most of
us live, the evening paper advertises 20 different films,
showing at perhaps 60 theatres, within a few minutes travel
time.

Further, there was almost no range of choice when it
came to education. In a small-town school of the 1940s, even
at the high school level, there were virtually no electives,
and we could never choose among two or more teachers
for a subject. To have diversity requires numbers—a scarce
commodity in small towns.

It should also be said that in some respects our range of
choices is narrowed, not broadened, by urbanization. Most
of us in large metropolises cannot choose at all whether we

will breathe clean air today. Many of us cannot choose to get away from large numbers of other people. We do not have the luxury of choosing to use in other ways those hours we give up each week for just traveling to and from work.

So urbanization has not been all gain in terms of enriching the choices open to persons. But I think we must still conclude that the options have been expanded by the urbanizing of our society.

The variety of choices available has increased also in the whole area of family planning. For most of human history, there were few choices to be made. If man and wife made love with a certain regularity, a certain number of conceptions would occur, a certain number of those conceptions would produce live births, and a certain number of the children born would live to adulthood. The only real element of choice involved the frequency of intercourse, and most human beings apparently have had little success in trying either to increase or to decrease the average regularity of that very basic human activity.

But now, just within the past decade, mankind has developed medical and technological capability making possible a whole series of fertility choices which did not exist before. Couples now can effectively decide (1) whether to have children at all, (2) if so, when to have them, (3) how many to have, (4) to have them by adoption rather than by procreation. In fact, even single persons may now choose to adopt children in many parts of the nation.

Because of changing law and practice regarding contraception, abortion, and voluntary sterilization, it is now possible, for those who wish it, to make separate decisions about fertility and sexual behavior. What once followed as a matter of course, no longer must, necessarily. The result is a vast expansion in the realm of choices to be made.

Geneticists suggest that fairly soon another set of choices will be thrust upon us—the capability of deciding what kinds of genetic design we wish to program into future offspring. I still find that prospect on the scary side.

Finally, in death prevention, too, the variety of choices is growing continually. People for centuries just died, and doctors or their predecessors were in attendance to make the dying as painless as possible. Now medicine must make choices about when to stop thwarting death, about who should get transplants or be plugged into expensive life-sustaining machines.

In many and sometimes fearsome ways, the scientific and technological development of mankind is pushing back the frontier so that the territory where chance operates is reduced and the territory where choice emerges is expanded. The quantity of choices we are asked to make is certain to increase.

Some Major Choices Facing All of Us

Let us now examine the way change has come to three life choices which confront every human being: the choice about a mate, the choice of life work, the choice of life style.

It is easy to see that the quality of choice open to most of us today concerning life mate is far greater than it was a generation or two ago. My high school graduating class, for example, had 10 girls. A number were committed to someone else and not really available for me; one or two were Roman Catholic, and in those days a faithful Lutheran wasn't supposed to consider marriage with one of *them;* some just didn't appeal to me. That left maybe two genuine possibilities in my entire graduating class. You could double the number by including the class just behind us, and still have a pretty thin lineup.

Now I realize that for millennia men and women chose one another (or had it done for them) from a range of options no more numerous, and some of them had happy marriages. I also realize that the proportion of happy marriages is probably no greater when the quantity of potential mates is increased. But it *seems* like a better arrangement to have as much diversity as is practical in the choice of a mate. The food is usually more enjoyable when ordered from a menu which seems unlimited. You don't eat any more, but you know that the long menu allowed you to be so much more discriminating!

I sense an increasing social acceptance also of the choice *not* to mate. In the past those who did not marry—women especially—were viewed as failures and social misfits. That attitude is relaxing, and we should welcome it.

Two major changes with respect to life work have come upon us in recent times. One is the obvious and almost overwhelming increase in the number of occupations available. Most men in the rural Midwest at the beginning of this century had two options: to stay on the farm or to take the drastic step of uprooting oneself to look for a factory job in some big city. Only a few were needed to run the shops, do the teaching, the doctoring, the lawyering, and the preaching for the great bulk of an agricultural community—those who worked the land.

It was assumed until recently that the one standard work role for women was housewife and mother. Clearly, that assumption has had it. New roles for women are emerging rapidly and the phenomenon is closely related to the fertility control choices discussed above. What some men do not yet seem to understand is that the redefinition of women's role will automatically redefine what it means to be a male. Or maybe a lot of men *do* understand this subconsciously and reject it because of the threat to male identity which it implies. In any case, the day is past when it was unnecessary to ask little girls, "What do you want to be when you grow up?"

The second big change concerning life work choices is that now very few of them are lifelong. The 40-year career, whether in farming, the ministry, teaching, even law or medicine, is becoming increasingly rare. Again, there is an expansion of freedom in this broadening of options. But it is at the same time threatening to one's security—both occupationally and psychologically. It appears that one's work life will never again be a settled thing, with one's decision about employment made by age 20 and the next 40 to 50 years spent in spinning out the consequences of that decision.

You run into a growing number of persons who talk about "my next career," without having any specific idea of what it might be or even where they might live in the pursuit of it. Some of this breed will tell you that a person should change jobs every three or four years—for his employer's sake as well as his own—and change careers every eight or ten.

Finally, a word about style of life, which is related to one's work but is broader: it has to do with one's total view of life.

Here too we are faced with a growing pluralism. It used to be that perhaps 99% of us were traditional in life style. Every small town had its eccentrics, those who departed from the conventional in behavior, but they were never numerous enough to be taken seriously or to constitute a true alternative and thus a threat. Now it is different.

Willis Elliott, an American theologian, sees at least four distinctive styles of life in presentday America. There is still the traditional, in which most of us continue to find ourselves; it is marked by what we conveniently call middle-class values, with strong emphasis on competition, achievement, acquisition of property, maintenance of economic security for me and mine.

Then he sees two sorts of radical life style emerging: the *mystic,* which prizes communion with fellowman, with nature, perhaps with God, as the supreme good (much of the early hippie movement had goals like these); and the *revolutionary,* which seeks justice as the highest good and is epitomized by the political activists who believe that commitment to change requires not just conventional political activity but *living* in a different way.

Dr. Elliott says the fourth life style is mixed. A growing number of persons and families in America show some evidences of all of the first three. It is a confused life style, but a rich one. He points out that the New Testament is like that: "it hasn't got its thing all together." The New Testament has a pluralism of themes, of emphases, of imperatives concerning how one ought to live in response to the gospel.

Maybe that is the one essential thing for Christians in our time to discover and to accept: that God not only permits pluralism, he delights in it.

Acceptance of that thoroughly biblical insight would bring a fullness to our choices and a sense of freedom to our choosing.

The Holy Spirit wears pants.—Stanley Graven in *Event* magazine, April 1970.

The specific task of the church in the modern world is the Christian celebration of change.—Ivan Illich in *Commentary*, April 1970.

6.

Churches and Choices

Collections of people, like individuals, need to make choices. One particular kind of collection of people is the church. The church is distinct from all other human institutions because of its origin (God's call) and its purpose (to help men live in the gospel). In all other respects, the church is like any human organization.

In other words, churches are *political* institutions—not political in the narrow sense of having the election and maintenance of public officials as their function, but political in the broad sense of having to do with the distribution of power and the making of decisions.

I suppose it is obvious that churches must make choices —about how best to use their resources, what aspect of the gospel message to emphasize at a given moment, how to behave in relation to the government and other institutions. Most Christians would agree that churches must be thoughtful in making these choices.

It has not always been so taken-for-granted, however, that churches need to be equally thoughtful about *how* the choices are made, about the process by which decisions in the churches are reached.

We need then to talk about two big subjects in this chapter: *how* churches make choices, and *what* are some of the current choices before the churches. Just to make it clear, we will be talking about church in all of its organized expressions: congregation, regional grouping, national denomination, and councils of churches from local to world level.

How Churches Make Choices—Theory

It still bothers some church members to talk openly and without shame about the church's politics. I suspect that's because the word "politics" in any context, including that of government and public affairs, is something of a dirty word. So, we conclude, it may be necessary to have some kind of politics, evil as it is, in the realm of the state, but let's keep it out of the church, for God's sake.

Such has been the conventional attitude of Christians in America. But that attitude is changing. One evidence of the change is the appearance of a book titled *Church Politics* by an American Lutheran theologian, Dr. Keith Bridston. Dr. Bridston argues that the church's reluctance to face openly the political character of its decision-making has not made politics in the church disappear. "Repression and denial of politics in the church has not done away with the political problems inherent in church life, but has made them more difficult to define and handle." [1]

Often, when Christians have wondered about how church decisions are made, their leaders have replied with some general word about "the guidance of the Holy Spirit." I remember as a boy hearing that the reason one candidate for a pastorate was called and not another was simply that Rev. So-and-So was the Holy Spirit's choice. In other versions, the Holy Spirit directed his servants (sometimes the bishop, sometimes the congregation) to make the right choice. Usually, of course, such choices are not made by chance. Either the ecclesiastical superior or the congregation knows something about the candidates, and that knowledge informs the decision.

Now, I believe that the guidance of the Holy Spirit is indeed involved in such choices. But I emphatically do *not* believe that the Holy Spirit functions best when the human beings participating in the choosing process are the most ignorant. The Holy Spirit is fully capable of working through and with the knowledge and judgment of human beings.

Stanley Graven, a physician and member of a national Lutheran mission board, has written: "The sad fact remains that there are many clergy who espouse, and even worse there are more laymen who swallow, the nonsense that decisions in the church are made through the Holy Spirit telling men how to vote when they know nothing of either side of the issue or the background qualifications and beliefs of the candidate."[2]

It seems to me that when we pray for the guidance of the Spirit in making such decisions, we are not asking him to do the choosing for us in some magical or mysterious way. We are asking for his guidance that we will use our own sense, weighing the total situation and making the decision according to the criteria which are appropriate to the divine purposes of the people of God.

Prayer, it has always seemed to me, is not a matter of getting answers directly from God in some flash-of-enlightenment manner—though that can happen on occasion. Rather, prayer for the Christian is putting oneself in an attitude of openness to the mind of Christ. And we all have at least *some* idea of what that means.

The agony of decision for the Christian includes the mental or psychological stance of openness to the divine mentality which we see reflected in Jesus. That does *not* mean if we approach decisions in an attitude of prayer we will always make the best ones, or even good ones. (If prayer could promise that, it would be a lot more popular!) Individuals and churches certainly ought to use prayer as part of the decision-making process—which is to say we should "put on the mind of Christ." But let no one think this will make the process less painful. Nor does it mean that because we have prayed about it we cannot make bad choices.

What I am saying is that there are thoroughly human factors involved in the decisions made by churches, and this is legitimate. Among other things, that means we can relax and stop feeling so uncomfortable when decisions have been clearly bad ones. It doesn't mean we have to defend such decisions, on the assumption that the Holy Spirit cannot make a mistake. It means churches too can make mistakes, sometimes big ones, because fallible human beings participate in the decisions.

How Churches Make Choices—Practice

So much for this rather hasty attempt to define a theory. There are a couple of practical matters concerned with the *how* which need mention.

The first is the matter of representation. The most glaring deficiency has to do with the rights of women. It has been pointed out that women have a majority at only one point in the life of the church: its basic membership. After that, at every representation level, women are outnumbered by men. In some denominations, women still do not have *any* representaton on local church boards. In others, they are barred from delegate status at national conventions of the denomination. In all they are vastly under-represented.

Dr. Elizabeth Farians, a Catholic theologian, says "it's all right if women come to church with a cake in their hands, but if they come with an idea in their heads they're not welcome."

Not long ago, I was a member of a congregation in which a new governing body of 12 members was to be selected. The chairman of the nominating committee announced that the slate included "a fair representation of women." There were four women and eight men on the slate. Granted, the ratio was an improvement over the congregation's previous practice and the practice of the great majority of churches in America. But in what sense was one seat out of three "fair" for women, who accounted for over 50% of the membership? The saddest part of the story is that the women too accepted this man's statement; at least none was moved to voice a protest or to contest the slate presented.

At the denominational level, women are beginning to challenge the "masculine mystique." Women delegates at a national meeting of the American Baptist Convention in 1970 presented a document showing that women held only 25% of the seats on national boards and committees and 21% of the professional staff positions of the denomination, and that opportunities for women clergy were severely limited.

The national convention of The American Lutheran Church in 1970 had four times as many women delegates as the previous convention in 1968—but they still totaled only 10% of the lay delegates.

In addition to the under-representation of women, there are other inequities in the power arrangements of the churches. Youth are now given the vote at around age 14 in a growing number of Protestant churches. The great majority, however, do not give youth a seat on official boards of local churches, nor are they seated as full delegates in most national conventions of churches. (The Lutheran World Federation Assembly in 1970 made a breakthrough on this score when it provided one official delegate seat out of seven for youth between the ages of 18 and 25.)

Of course, *all* age groups should be properly represented. Although older people should perhaps be better represented because of their experience, we have given a disproportionate voice to age. Sometimes more than half the lay representatives at conventions have been over age 65—because retired people had time they were willing to give!

Maybe the toughest issue of representation is the appropriate ratio of clergy and laity at all levels. In most of American Christianity, it is only at the local church level that lay persons have a majority voice. As soon as one moves to a non-local level of the structure, the ratio traditionally has been equally divided between clergy and laity. At its worst, it can still be predominantly clergy, but this pattern is changing.

What then would be a proper ratio? At the extreme, it has been argued that the ratio should follow the actual numerical situation of the denomination. If, for example, a denomination of 2 million adult members has 6,000 clergymen, that's a ratio of three clergymen per thousand. A national convention of 1,000 delegates would be composed of 997 lay men and women and three pastors.

Both you and I know that such a formula is not going to be adopted. And there are some good reasons why it should not be. The most important have to do with the special education and experience of those 6,000 clergymen. To put it crassly, the contribution and influence of each pastor will inevitably weigh more heavily than that of each lay person. The question is, should the system continue to allow each clergy voice to count as much as 333 lay voices?

How would you feel about some formula like the following? Let delegate conventions be three-fourths lay, one-fourth clergy. And is there any good reason why the lay portion cannot always be half women and half men? Further, about 20% of the lay portion ought to be composed of youth in the 15-25 bracket. That would give our mythical convention of 1,000 delegates this breakdown:

250 clergymen
375 lay men (75 of them age 25 and under)
375 lay women (75 of them 25 and under)

For policy-setting boards and committees, apart from the local level, how about one-third clergy, one-third lay women, one-third lay men? (The American Lutheran Church in 1970 decided to make all of its national boards one-third clergy and two-thirds laity.) If about 20% of the lay persons were youth, that would put one young person on a board of nine, two on a board of 15.

Local church governing boards, unless a very unusual male/female ratio exists in the congregation as a whole, ought to be half men and half women. And a board of 12 persons should include one *young* woman and one *young* man (25 or under).

The other practical consideration I wish to raise concerns the way we handle elections in the church. There have been several elements in the traditional procedure which could stand serious reassessment:

1. *The custom, in probably the great majority of local church elections, of listing only one nominee for each position to be filled.* There are two chief reasons for this practice, as I see it. First the desire to avoid a contest and the possibility of resulting hard feelings. My answer to that is we would be much healthier as an institution if we could behave like mature human beings who accept contesting as part of any election process. The fabric binding us together

in the fellowship of the church should be strong enough
to take it. If it isn't, perhaps we need to find that out. A
second reason for having only one name on the ballot is
said to be the difficulty of finding even one who will con-
sent to run. Again, something else may be wrong. Where
a position is viewed as significant, in terms of opportunity
for influence or accomplishment, it is seldom difficult to find
candidates. Perhaps having local church elections contested
would suggest that the positions are important enough to
be worth contesting for. The chief reason why more than
one name should be offered, of course, is that it gives those
voting a measure of choice. They are not then merely
ratifiers of what a small group—the nominating committee
—proposed. They can do some choosing themselves.

2. *The thesis that candidates ought not offer themselves
for ecclesiastical office.* "The job should seek the man, not
the man the job," is the usual way of putting it. No one is
distressed when candidates actively pursue governmental
elective office, but the same behavior disturbs many if the
object is elective office in the church. I suppose the reason
is that we have felt it unseemly for persons to aspire to an
office which is identified with holiness. However, we know
that leaders and potential leaders in the church, just as
elsewhere, are human, with all the normal attributes of
drive and ambition—and those are not necessarily negative
characteristics. Further, there's more help than harm in
having a variety of persons who believe they have the particular leadership ability required for an office willing to
say so and to make themselves available.

3. *The almost total lack of political organizing, at least in the open.* It is foolish to pretend that delegates to a national church convention will find out about the candidates and the issues entirely on their own initiative. The best thing to be said for organized campaigning is that it puts the initiative where it belongs, with those who feel strongly about an issue or a candidate and who wish to organize in order to spread the word. An ecclesiastical code of fair campaign practices would be a good thing, no doubt. But within such a set of guidelines, political activity of all sorts should be permitted and encouraged for national and probably state or regional church elections. Not only would church elections then be more educative, they'd also be more interesting.

Clearly, there are other viewpoints on the above issues. I'm proposing what I feel would be an improvement. You may see other ways, but I hope you'll agree that some changes in our church election procedures are needed.

Some Choices Before the Churches

Even before we get our procedural problems taken care of, we have some decisions to make as churches. These are decisions that are being made continuously, every time a congregation adopts a yearly budget, whenever a national denomination reviews its program emphases. In the second half of this chapter, we shall look at just three areas in which choices for the churches are especially pressing these days: our relation to the state, our relation to our own economic strength, and the continuing need to determine our priorities.

Our relation to the state as churches in America promises to become more troublesome in the immediate future. Churches in this country have enjoyed a position of institutional privilege for most of our history. That is, the policy of the government with regard to religious institutions has been one which could be called "benign neutrality." No other institutions have enjoyed quite the same status in our system. In many respects, the policy has worked well. It has certainly allowed the religious institutions to operate with a great measure of freedom, and to become relatively strong in economic and organizational terms.

But more and more Christians see a serious problem in the privileged status which churches in America enjoy. They see the religious institutions tempted to remain silent on major issues involving the state, lest their special position in relation to government to jeopardized. They see the development of a milder form of the "silent church" situation which Germany knew during the Hitler days.

There are two good examples of our privileged position as churches in the United States these days. One is our special tax situation. The other concerns exemption from military service for our students of theology and clergymen.

The tax situation has several elements. Generally across the country we pay no taxes of any kind on property used for worship and education. In most states and communities, we pay no property taxes on parsonages and other housing occupied by professional church employees. In some states, even income-producing property owned by a religious organization remains tax-exempt. Finally, there are income tax breaks given to the clergy which result in another form of special privilege to religious institutions (we can pay less in salaries than an ordinary employer without reducing the employee's take-home pay).

All who have studied the problem recognize a form of subsidy from the general society to institutional religion in all of these tax exemptions. But not all agree that the subsidies are equally questionable. In my view, it is no longer possible to justify federal income tax exemption on that portion of clergy income which is spent for housing. Why should just one of all occupational groups—those who happen to be ecclesiastically employed—pay no tax on income which is designated as housing allowance? If actual housing is provided, rather than a housing allowance, the same principle ought to apply. We estimate the value of provided housing for purposes of assessing church pension; why not also for income tax purposes? Then let the employer (local church, national boards, or whatever) pay a decent enough salary that the church employee may be taxed like everyone else. Anything less than this is demeaning to the office of the church employee, and to the church as an institution, since it suggests that special treatment is necessary. In a way, it puts church employees "on welfare," since public funds are being permitted to provide a portion of the salary which the church employer ought to assume fully.

Likewise, buildings used to house our employees and property used to produce income should be taxed just as any similar property not church-owned would be. Why should a piece of real property occupied by a minister's family contribute nothing toward local school needs through the property tax, for example? In many states this is still the case, though state legislatures are having a new look at the whole tax-exemption picture. We ought to be letting our lawmakers know that we no longer need or want privileged treatment for the church as an organization.

Some local churches are voluntarily making payments to school districts and municipalities "in lieu of taxes" on their worship and education property—based on two major considerations. First, the churches cost the local communities money just by being there, directly by consuming services (including the education of the pastor's children), and indirectly by keeping property off the tax rolls. The second consideration is simply the pressing revenue shortage of local government, which needs every bit of help it can get.

I'm not talking about church property used for worship or education purposes—only that used for housing or to produce income. And regarding the question of church/state separation, we are in relationship unavoidably when it comes to tax matters. Either churches and church employees pay certain taxes like everyone else (which we already do in many situations), or we continue, in effect, to receive subsidies from government which, to my mind, are increasingly hard to justify. We cannot escape some form of church-state involvement on taxes.

Regarding the draft, most of the pressure to rethink our historic acceptance of exemption for professional clergy is coming from those most directly affected: young men in seminaries. Let me quote from a statement which 101 students at Lutheran School of Theology at Chicago sent to the president of the Lutheran Church in America in 1970, asking him to press before a congressional committee for an end to the clergy deferment provision of Selective Service law:

> We maintain that automatic exemption for clergy-men reinforces distorted notions of church and ministry, and that it leads to an artificial barrier between men engaged in a common faith and mission. . . .
>
> The national policy of granting special privileges to the church, such as the exemption of clergy, tempts the church into a position of ineffectual silence on controversial issues.
>
> We are convinced that the church's witness for peace is weakened because its ministers have not directly come to terms with the problems of taking part in conscription and war. The surrender of moral decision to military authority, the destruction of human life, and the ambiguity of justice in armed conflict are all peripheral, academic questions for an exempted clergy.[3]

The general attitude of the American public concerning special privileges for religious institutions appears to be moving toward elimination of at least certain of the privileges. Governments are reluctant to change the laws granting privileges until the institutions which benefit show that they will welcome such changes. But if the public pressure for changes becomes great enough, lawmakers will have no choice. I believe it is far preferable for the religious groups themselves to initiate the discussion and press for legitimate corrections, as many of them are now doing.

If we have a servant understanding of the church's role in the world, we will find it legitimate to apply that understanding to matters like tax policy and draft deferment for our professional employees. If we believe the church has a divine right to a privileged position in relation to the state, then we will resist changes in the present relationship. Wherever we stand, there are choices we will soon need to be making around issues like these. May our decisions be informed ones!

A related but much broader issue concerns *our own economic power.*

As institutions, the religious groups of America account for more purchasing power than any other entity except the federal government. How they use that power has a lot to do with the maintenance or reform of the other structures and systems of American society. The churches may choose to make no basic change in how we deploy our institutional money power. Or we may choose to go in substantially new directions. In either case, our choices will have great consequences, both for the shape of the society in which we live and in expressing the soul of the churches. Let me pose as questions some of the new choices:

Will the churches be willing to yield control over significant portions of their resources (annual income or property or both) and transfer that capital to self-determining community groups struggling for social, racial, and economic justice—without keeping strings on how the money is used?

Will the churches be willing to reconsider their use of property, perhaps selling some and putting the land or income to social uses, sharing existing facilities across denominational lines (since we have plenty of buildings already but they're mostly under-used), opening up our buildings to community uses as part of a servant stance toward the society, and building no new buildings until all other alternatives have been explored?

Will the churches at the national level be willing to change their investment policies, so that return-on-investment is not the overriding consideration, being balanced against concern for the investment's social impact (which means looking at an industry's balance sheet in relation to perpetuating the military system, environmental destruction, and economic or racial injustice)?

Will the churches—to put it all into a single question—voluntarily become poorer as part of their servanthood in this hour, following their Lord who, though rich, made himself poor in order to become the servant of all?

We might remember, as someone has said, that the orthodoxy of a congregation can be read more powerfully in its annual statement of accounts than in its weekly statement of beliefs.

About What We're About

All the foregoing questions and choices are a part of the really basic issue before the church: *what is the whole thing for anyway?*

Every generation of Christians needs to decide what the church is *primarily* for in its time. To put it another way, which of the many emphases in the gospel does the world most need today? We have that old guideline from the preacher who said his sermons were faithful to the divine revelation if they both comforted the afflicted and afflicted the comfortable. The church is always called to be simultaneously pastoral and prophetic; to be with people at their points of pain and crises, and to work for change in human systems which cause pain and crises; to bring healing to the oppressed and judgment to the oppressor. How do we speak meaningfully of this today?

Perhaps the dominant theme among theologians in recent decades has been that of humanization, the making human of all aspects of life. The church's task, as they describe it, is to work for the humanizing of existence under, in, and through the lordship of Jesus Christ. This paragraph from the World Council of Churches study on missionary congregations expresses it well:

> The New Testament provides a variety of messianic images which denote the goal of God's mission. . . . We have lifted up humanization as the goal of mission because we believe that more than others it communicates in our history the meaning of the messianic goal. In another time the goal of God's redemptive work might best have been described in terms of man turning toward God, rather than in terms of God turning toward man. . . . Today the fundamental question is much more that of true man, and the dominant concern of the missionary congregation must therefore be to point to the humanity in Christ as the goal of mission.[4]

Albert Camus, the French novelist and a non-Christian, said the world looked to the church for something which could come only from the church. Some time after World

War II, he wrote these words, which if anything are more meaningful today than when first uttered:

> For a long time during those frightful Nazi years I waited for a great voice to speak up in Rome. I, an unbeliever? Precisely. For I knew that the spirit would be lost if it did not utter a cry of condemnation when faced with force. . . . What the world expects of Christians is that Christians should speak out loud and clear and that they should voice their condemnation in such a way that never a doubt, never the slightest doubt, could rise in the heart of the simplest man. That they should get away from abstractions and confront the bloodstained face history has taken on today.[5]

Another description of the church's primary task for this moment in history comes from Ivan Illich, Roman Catholic director of a mission training center in Cuernevaca, Mexico. He writes, "The specific task of the church in the modern world is the Christian celebration of the experience of change."[6]

Illich does not put the stress on the church working to bring about change. He does not deny that some of that activity is necessary. But he prefers to stress the role of *celebrating* change, lifting it up as the essence of contemporary existence and giving it meaning, helping people not to be afraid of change but to welcome it as bringing promise and zest and development and renewal to human life. Change, after all, is the stuff of which life is composed. Christians, because of the substance and the images of the gospel, have the resources to do this job for the world, Illich says, and the world badly needs to have the job done.

Illich's suggestion is easier said than done. Much of our traditional emphasis in the church has been to glorify the opposite of change. Through many centuries, the Western church has suggested that the ideal situation is to find peace in a God who changes not. The strong implication was that if God does not change, he must be as uncomfortable with change as we are. He therefore must be on the side of those who would maintain the status quo. As one illustration of the innocent way in which such images are buttressed, consider these lines from a well-loved hymn:

> "In heavenly love abiding,
> No change my heart shall fear;
> And safe is such confiding,
> For nothing changes here."

It will not be easy to develop the celebration of change when for centuries we have had a theology exalting unchange as an ideal.

Finally, we can speak of the church's task as the opposite of problem-solving. The world needs a church which can provide meaning for all those problems of human beings which will never be solved. No matter how just a society we may strive to build, there will still be problems. People will continue to suffer in one way or another. Sin will survive. Mankind will never have arrived, in any utopian sense. There will continue to be cruelty and alienation and despair. There will be death.

We need a church which can major in ministering to people caught up in problems which cannot be solved. As Dean M. Kelley has written, "The special subject matter for religious meanings is not the problems men can manage if they try hard enough, but those they *can't* manage however hard they try: handicaps, suffering, death." [7]

It is the Anglo-Saxon's manifest destiny to go forth as a world conqueror. . . .This is what fate holds for the chosen people.—William Allen White in the *Emporia* (Kansas) *Gazette,* 1898

Either you will join the ranks of suffering and humiliation — beginning perhaps with "losing face" in Vietnam— or there will be no "chosen people" on these shores.—Vincent Harding, 1967

7.

Hard Choices for a "Chosen Nation"

Our Chosen Nation Mentality

This will be a hard section to read. It is also hard to write. Hard meaning painful.

To speak of the choosing we must now do as an American people, we need to review some of the choosing we have done in the past. We must see that many of our past choices were shaped by a Chosen Nation complex. I believe that we cannot constructively make the necessary national choices until we shed our Chosen Nation mentality.

The Hebrew Scriptures tell how the Israelites wanted repeatedly to pervert their relationship with God into a kind of divine justification for whatever the nation wanted to do. The Lutheran theologian William Hordern writes:

> We have been developing in America precisely that sort of folk-religion that Amos, Hosea, Isaiah, and Jeremiah so bitterly condemned. We speak glibly

about "this nation under God," but how often do we
mean "this nation under God's judgment"? We identify religion and patriotism so closely that instead of
trying diligently to find God's will for us, we assume
that what we want for ourselves must be what God
wants us to have. There can be no more sinister heresy than this one.[1]

From the time our Anglo-Saxon founding fathers arrived
along the Atlantic Coast, our national myth has been one
of righteousness, innocence, and "manifest destiny." We
have, from the beginning, believed that the nation to be
built here by transplanted Europeans was destined to provide a new birth of political and economic freedom for all
of mankind. We were destined, *chosen,* for that role. We
believed that Americans were really less capable of national
greed and self-seeking than other nations. We were con-
vinced that Providence intended for us to occupy the continent from Atlantic to Pacific, and then to extend the
blessings of the "American way of life" around the entire
globe.

The tragedy is that in many ways and for many decades,
America *did* hold the brightest promise for the beleaguered
millions of this planet. And that fact blinded most of us to
what we were doing in the process of extending our power
and influence, first across this continent and then across
the oceans.

We were able to destroy and enslave other people, at first,
because we drew a distinct line between "civilized" and
"uncivilized" peoples. Later, our national prestige and
power were at stake. Our innocence and sense of chosen-

ness lasted for more than 300 years, and it was not until the present national crisis over racism and militarism that large numbers of us have really pondered the dark side of our history and the legacy it has handed us.

A history of colonial Massachusetts reports that the European settlements early came to view the nearby Pequot Indians as their enemy. In May 1637, a military force under Captain John Mason surprised the chief town of the Pequots near Saybrook in a night attack, shooting down every Indian who sought to leave the village, and slowly burning alive the 500 men, women and children who remained inside. A renowned Protestant minister of that day, Dr. Cotton Mather, furnishes this written summary of the massacre: "It was supposed that no less than six hundred heathen Pequot souls were brought down to hell that day." [2]

If those you kill are heathen (that is, not "God's chosen"), it appears to be less of a crime to eliminate them. They would, after all, be going to hell anyway in the end.

But killing was not the only way of getting the Indian out of our path. As Governor Gilmore of Georgia wrote in 1830: "Treaties were expedients by which ignorant, intractable, and savage people were induced without bloodshed to yield up what civilized peoples had a right to possess." [3]

John C. Calhoun was no redneck rabble-rouser. A senator, cabinet member, and vice-president of the United States, he was widely respected as an honorable and righteous man, from pious Presbyterian stock, and educated at Yale. He merely expressed what many, perhaps most, Americans (North and South) believed in the middle third of the 19th century, when he said: "What is called slavery is in reality a political institution, essential to the peace, safety and prosperity of those states of the Union in which it exists." Calhoun also said that slavery was "instead of evil, a good—a positive good." And not only for the slaveholder, but for the enslaved as well: " . . . in no other condition, or in any other age or country, has the Negro race ever attained so high an elevation in morals, intelligence, or civilization." [4]

As black Americans have long known and whites are finding out, the Civil War changed little. Note this statement by a Congregational clergyman, Josiah Strong, in his 1885 book, *Our Country: Its Possible Future and Its Present Crises:* "[The superior Anglo-Saxon people is destined] to dispossess many weaker races, assimilate others, and mold the remainder, until, in a very true and important sense, it has Anglo-Saxonized mankind." [5]

The impulse to take civilization to mankind's "lesser breeds" remained strong among our politicians as well. A few years after the Rev. Mr. Strong's book appeared, Senator Albert Beveridge of Indiana, in only slightly less exclusive rhetoric, exclaimed: "God has not been preparing the English-speaking and Teutonic peoples for a thousand years for nothing but vain and idle self-admiration. No! He has made us the master organizers of the world to establish system where chaos reigns. . . . He has made us adept in government that we may administer government among savages and senile peoples." [6]

It wasn't long before such sentiments were translated into the expansionist logic of war. We found one in 1898 with Spain. The goal of the war, for many Americans, was to extend around the globe the influence of God's new chosen people. The task was stated clearly by William Allen White, famed editor of Kansas' *Emporia Gazette:* "Only Anglo-Saxons can govern themselves. The Cubans will need a despotic government for many years to restrain anarchy until Cuba is filled with Yankees. . . . It is the Anglo-Saxon's manifest destiny to go forth as a world conqueror. He will take possession of the islands of the sea. . . . This is what fate holds for the chosen people. It is so written. . . . It is to be." [7]

President William McKinley, in late 1898, summed up in a single magnificent statement the rationale for that beginning of American imperialism. Concerning what to do with the Philippine Islands, McKinley wrote that he " . . . prayed almighty God for light and guidance. . . . And one night late it came to me . . . (1) that we could not give them back to Spain—that would be cowardly and dishonorable; (2) that we could not turn them over to France or Germany—our commercial rivals in the Orient—that would be bad business and discreditable; (3) that we could not leave them to themselves—they were unfit for self-government . . . and (4) that there was nothing left for us to do but to take them all, and to educate the Filipinos, and uplift and civilize and Christianize them, and by God's grace do the very best we could by them, as our fellowmen for whom Christ also died." [8]

Not all Filipinos accepted the kind intentions of the United States. A guerilla war raged for a couple of years, and widespread dissent developed within American society. Even an industrial tycoon such as Andrew Carnegie became distressed, to the point where he could write to a friend in McKinley's administration: "You seem to have about finished your work of civilizing the Filipinos; it is thought that about 8,000 of them have been completely civilized and sent to Heaven." [9]

Our special attitude toward Orientals showed up again 40 years later, when we found ourselves at war with Japan and couldn't bring ourselves to trust the Japanese-Americans in our midst. We were at war with Germany and Italy too, but German-Americans and Italian-Americans were left alone. Japanese-Americans we herded into concentration camps—"evacuation centers" we called them. The story has not been told often enough. This summary appears in Grodzins' *Americans Betrayed:*

> One hundred ten thousand Americans of Japanese ancestry were evacuated. . . . No charges were ever filed against these persons and no guilt ever attributed to them. The test was ancestry applied with the greatest rigidity. Evacuation swept into guarded camps orphans, foster children in white homes, Japanese married to Caucasians, the off-spring of Japanese ancestry, and American citizens with as little as one-sixteenth Japanese blood. Evacuation was not carried out by lawless vigilantes or by excited local officials. The program was instituted and executed by military forces of the U.S. with a full mandate of power from both the executive and legislative branches of the national government. [10]

While fighting Hitler's racist doctrines, we applied a similar test to certain of our own citizens, not one of whom was ever found to have committed any disloyal act. The racial nature of our fear was expressed openly by a General Dewitt in testimony before a sub-committee of the House Naval Affairs Committee on April 13, 1943:

> It makes no difference whether he is an American citizen, he is still a Japanese. American citizenship does not necessarily determine loyalty. You need not worry about the Italians at all except in certain cases. Also, the same for the Germans except in individual cases. But we must worry about the Japanese all the time until he is wiped off the map.[11]

Our record for 350 years has been pretty much the same: if a group of people looks different or has a distinctly different culture, we are justified in treating them as our inferiors. There is little doubt that some of our attitude stemmed from simple racism, drawing assumptions of superiority on the basis of physical difference. But a part of it also came from our profound belief that we were *chosen* to impress our ways, our values, our definition of civilization on the rest of the world.

Through both world wars in the first half of the 20th century, there was a dual impulse driving American participation. On the one hand, we were motivated to help stamp out totalitarian systems which threatened to extend their power throughout the world. On the other hand, there was also a desire to replace one would-be world-embracing system with another: the American way of life.

From Threat to Hope Again?

For a long time, most of us assumed rather unthinkingly that, if they had the choice, the rest of the world would choose the American way. We were for self-determination by other peoples, but we figured that meant they would choose political and economic systems modeled after ours. After World War II, we were naively confident that the so-called uncommitted peoples (that is, not aligned with either the Western allies or the Soviet-Chinese bloc) would want to be like us, build institutions like ours, and join our side in battling the Communists.

It has come as a shock to discover, with gradual awareness through the Cold War '50s and early '60s, and with stunning suddenness since our Southeast Asian war, that the new nations are far from wanting America as their model. Indeed, more and more of the world's nations, including our longtime friends in the Western family, are telling us that the world no longer sees us as its messianic expectation, as its "last best hope," though indeed much of the world once did.

We ourselves began to believe that, in becoming the most powerful nation economically and militarily, we had the credentials for shaping the world in our image. We too fell for the deception that "might is right." The country which once held the greatest promise for the world now seemed to hold the most terror. The turning point in our self-understanding began with the Vietnam escalation of the mid-'60s and the subsequent reassessment of national goals and purposes.

Voices from outside have helped us to see ourselves in a new way. Let me cite several analyses, not from those hostile to America, but from friends who have lived among us and still see hope for us. In 1970, Arnold J. Toynbee, the British historian, wrote:

> To most Europeans, I guess, America now looks like the most dangerous country in the world. Since America is unquestionably the most powerful country, the transformation of America's image within the last 30 years is very frightening for Europeans. It is probably still more frightening for the great majority of the human race who are neither Europeans nor North Americans, but are Latin Americans, Asians, and Africans. They, I imagine, feel even more insecure than we feel. They feel that, at any moment, America may intervene in their internal affairs with the same appalling consequences as have followed from American intervention in Southeast Asia.
>
> . . . The roles of America and Russia have been reversed in the world's eyes. Today America has become the world's nightmare. Like Communist Russia, America has committed atrocities in the cause of truth and justice as she sees them. . . . In terms of the number of lives taken and of lands laid waste, America's score is, unhappily, far greater than any other country's since the end of World War II.
>
> . . . How is America dealing with her problems? As we see it, she is failing to deal with them, and this is the most terrifying feature of American life today. . . . The American home front is more crucial than the ports in Vietnam and Cambodia and Taiwan and Korea and the Middle East. The decision on America's home front is going to decide the fate of the world, and the rest of us can do nothing about it. We have no say, but we too are going to be victims of America's domestic agony." [12]

Echoing that last thought—that the options and choices now being hammered out within American society are worldwide in consequence—is Dr. Paul Verghese, an Indian theologian. This world churchman, former staff member of the World Council of Churches and present member of its Central Committee, is principal of a Syrian Orthodox seminary in Kerala. He knows the United States well: he studied here, worked several years in the North Atlantic setting, and has traveled extensively in the West. At the beginning of the 1970s, he spoke these words to a group of U.S. church leaders:

> Your society is sick. But it is still the most creative society we have. . . . So this is why I still come back and talk to you. Because from you must come some sparks, because you still have a position in the world where you can lead the thinking of other people in the world. You set patterns. Your ideas catch on. That's why yours is still a creative society. And therefore you have a responsibility. But you perhaps sometimes may need some help from some of us, and if you will accept it with a little bit of dignity, I think it will be good.[13]

If Verghese and Toynbee are right—that the United States has become the world's chief threat but at the same time remains the place where mankind's future will essentially be decided——then we need not despair. The future is still open-ended. This is the only proper Christian view of history, after all: that there *is* hope because God's resurrection power continues to be present.

I believe that America is now prepared for a period of renewed health, is potentially on the road back to internal healing. After World War II the German Christians talked about their society having reached *Nullpunkt*—Point Zero. Their insight was that only after an arrogant and destructive people has been brought down to the very bottom can it see itself as it is, make repentance, and begin to reenter constructively the family of nations.

The trauma of the late 1960s and early '70s in America can have great healing power for us if we can see it as God's way of bringing us to our knees. We may not have come the same route as Germany, humbled through military defeat, although some of us believe we have been at least embarrassed if not humiliated in Southeast Asia. But our primary humbling has come through turmoil at home, the profound questioning of what America is for, the painful effort to redefine our national purpose and self-understanding, the honesty of seeing in the mirror our very great failure to reflect the ideals we have proclaimed for two centuries, the often violent clash between those who would change us more quickly and those who see change as un-American. It has all added up to the death of our Chosen Nation fantasy.

Our National Choices

Americans lived in a dream world for a long time. I think never again will that comfortable fantasy be possible for us. Part of the fantasy was that America was invincible on the battlefield. Maybe we have needed the experience of failure

in war because of the effect it would have on our own soul.
This perhaps is the lesson of Vietnam. I think Vincent
Harding, a black Christian theologian, is exactly on the
point when he relates our acceptance of humiliation abroad
and our trauma at home. Writing to whites back in 1967,
he said:

> Either you will join the ranks of suffering and hu-
> miliation—beginning perhaps with "losing face" in
> Vietnam—or there will be no "chosen people" on these
> shores. Either you will submit your children to some
> of the same educational terrors you have allowed black
> children to endure, or there is no future for any. Either
> you will give up your affluence to provide necessities
> for others, or there will be neither affluence nor neces-
> sities for anyone. Perhaps we were chosen together,
> and we cannot move towards a new beginning until
> we have faced all the horror and agony of the past
> and the present with absolute honesty.[14]

In that prophetic paragraph, Vincent Harding has outlined the nature of the choices open to America at this
moment:

We can choose first to stop fancying ourselves the chosen
people of the earth, with a God-given right to impose our
ways on others.

We can choose to funnel our wealth into the development
of peoples—according to *their* visions—rather than into
more and better instruments of destruction.

Finally we can choose to continue the original American
revolution, whose goal was to keep the power and the

wealth always distributed as fairly as human society can make possible.

Another way of speaking about the basic national choice is by telling a story. It has been around in various versions for some time. This one comes through Richard J. Neuhaus, a Lutheran pastor in Brooklyn. It concerns another world somewhere out in space, very much like our own. The people in it live under a variety of economies and political systems; they are divided into various ethnic, religious, and color groups.

They are different from earthlings in just one respect: within all the subgroups there is a total obsession with the welfare of mankind.

One result is that over 60% of their national budgets are poured into a compulsive crusade to shelter life from the normal ravages of existence. Governments spend billions on the conquest of disease. Medical research has had such large resources available that today no cancer or other degenerative disease exists. At the same time, population control programs have been so adequately funded that the threat of too many people is non-existent.

Vast sums are spent by government on housing. Fiscal policies are so structured that blight and slums are unprofitable and therefore unheard of. The education of children is considered so important that teachers are very well paid, so that teacher training schools can turn away all but the most qualified candidates.

But there is a perverseness in the totality of their obsession with welfare. It reaches its height in legislation against all private efforts in behalf of meeting human need. The outlawing of private charity, of course, tends to stifle the philanthropic instincts of the people.

There is but one outlet for this instinct. Private benevolence is permitted for one purpose only: national defense. The nation's budgets are so swollen with appropriations for human welfare that it is necessary for citizens privately to raise money for arms and armies.

Voluntary organizations have been established for just this purpose. People stand with tin cups on street corners collecting coins to buy carbines. There are clubs to finance uniforms, grenades, and tanks through dances and raffles. There are tag-days for military jets.

The inescapable fact is that the national governments have simply abandoned the matter of defense and left it entirely up to private agencies. But the inadequacy of the system is apparent to all. People are grumbling that under such a policy there will never be a war.

Will such a time ever come to Planet Earth? Will Americans again decide that it can be both patriotic and moral to choose butter over guns, housing over armies, education systems over ABM systems? President Eisenhower voiced his confidence in that hope in 1959 when the cold war mentality was still very much alive: "I like to believe that people in the long run are going to do more to promote peace than are governments. Indeed, I think that people want peace so much that one of these days governments had better get out of their way and let them have it."

Our Choices in Community

In this section I want to deal with two specific problems related to public decision-making within America. One is the problem of continuing to have choices made *by* some of us *for* others of us. The other is the problem of defining community appropriately for the issue, so that intelligent choices can be made.

The first problem is expressed in rhyme by Kenneth E. Boulding:

> The reason why cities are ugly and sad
> Is not that the people who live there are bad;
> It's that most of the people who really decide
> What goes on in the city live somewhere outside.[15]

It is now a truism that the people should be allowed to participate in making the decisions which affect their lives. We haven't made the changes in our political structures to translate the principle into practice. And we won't until the unrepresented demand that it change.

It's beginning to happen. Women are demanding that they be given the power to participate, along with male legislators and male physicians, in decisions involving the possibility of life within their own bodies. Young men are demanding that they be allowed to vote in the process which decides whether, when, and where they shall kill other young men. City dwellers are demanding that non-residents stop shaping the city's decisions, or start paying taxes for the privilege.

There are people among us, "trouble-makers" all, who

would change the power arrangements by which we have lived. When they are pushing for the justice of empowerment, the Christian can only say "power to you." And that means a willingness to share some of my power if I am over-empowered. Incidentally, you probably are if you fall into any of these categories:

> male
> white
> past 30
> annual salary in five figures

Some of us find ourselves under pressure to yield in all four directions at once. And that hurts.

The other problem, defining community in terms appropriate to the issue on which a choice must be made, is related to empowerment. But it has to do also with geography.

There are two pressures which appear to be counterproductive in America just now, resulting from different aspects of the same urban crisis.

One argues for centralization of decision-making. It usually calls for spreading the results of a decision over a larger territory. You include a city and its satellite suburbs and call it metropolitanization. You spread the power of a decision into two or more states and call it regionalization.

It is clear that something like metropolitanization or regionalization is needed to attack issues like air and water pollution or transportation or equitable tax policies.

But wait a minute, argue others. The problem is that we already have too much centralization; the units of government are already too large. We need to *de*-centralize. We need decisions made closer to the people, in communities of a size they can identify with.

The truth is, of course, that both are correct. We need to go both larger and smaller at the same time, toward both broader and more limited definitions of community, depending on the issue. It appears that this is beginning to happen in America, but the pace needs to be speeded up. And that requires an understanding of the problem which most of us do not yet have.

The best way to describe the situation is by examples.

There are certain "local" issues which even our largest cities, and often entire states, cannot handle. By itself, no central city in America can really make mass transit decisions that will solve anything, even if all the money in the world were available. This of course is because there are large numbers of commuters whose daily trips begin and end outside the territory of the central city. This means some kind of metropolitan authority must be created, with scope of territory broad enough to encompass the natural transportation community, which may include parts of three states as it does in metropolitan New York City.

Likewise, decisions regarding pollution control must be operative within a "natural pollution district," if there is such a thing. That means Missouri and Illinois getting together to handle the air pollution around greater St. Louis, and several states (or the federal government) policing the preservation of our major lakes and rivers.

At the same time, those public services which are especially close to the people served—like schools, police protection, health and welfare services—must be shaped in relatively small units.

The natural community for a public school system may include no more than 30,000 to 50,000 persons—large enough to support a good senior high school, a couple of junior high schools, and a half dozen elementary schools. This is precisely what the typical suburban community is, so the de-centralization of large central city school systems has been called the "suburbanization" of the big city.

The same kind of logic can be applied to police services. Police/community relations have become so sensitive that it is essential for citizens and police to know one another, or at least for citizens to feel they have control because the scale is small enough.

Urban analysts believe this is one of the factors in the development of suburbia. People like to live in political units small enough that there is some sense of potential influence. It is simply a statistical fact that the voice and vote of a person in Park Ridge, Illinois, is 100 times as big as that of his neighbor across the street in Chicago. Park Ridge has less than 40,000 persons; Chicago somewhat under 4 million. Each has an independent school system and police force.

With transit and pollution, we can't afford the luxury of "suburbanized" decision making. Fragmented decisions on such issues make no sense, either in terms of natural system or human sensitivity.

With services like education and police work, however, we can no longer afford *not* to break up the massive urban units. Chicago parents have a right to the same degree of influence as Park Ridge parents in the running of their schools.

One final word of caution: if decision-making structures in this country follow the pattern here outlined, we will need to abandon one of our most cherished fiscal theories. It is the belief that local tax money should be spent in the unit where it is collected. That is, we should not take tax dollars from relatively rich areas and spend them in relatively poorer areas, unless the rich and poor areas are in the same spending district.

But we are doing it increasingly in some states, where for education needs especially money collected at the state level is portioned out according to need, not according to the wealth which happens to be present within the local district.

The principle is growing. Some day soon, we will likely have large amounts of federally collected tax money distributed to the states without too many strings attached. In education particularly, the pressure for more money is so severe and the interdependence of the nation so great that we must seriously consider financing public schools increasingly from the federal level while retaining control at the state and local levels. This will inevitably mean some tax dollars from Minnesota flowing downstream to Mississippi. The alternative is to continue shipping north the products of Mississippi's inadequately financed education system.

This analysis has focused largely on structures for decision-making in our nation and our communities. The choices before us, also in this area, are hard ones because they mean a shifting of power and of money. But Vincent Harding's word comes back again:

"Either you will give up your affluence to provide necessities for others, or there will be neither affluence nor necessities for anyone. Perhaps we were chosen together, and we cannot move towards a new beginning until we have faced all the horror and agony of the past and the present with absolute honesty."

Eventually, it resolves itself into a choice between money and trees. If we choose the money (no matter how polite a name we give it), we lose the trees.—Lewis Lapham in *Harpers*, May 1970

The future is a cruel hoax. . . . I am terribly saddened by the fact that the most humane thing for me to do is to have no children at all.—Stephanie Mills, 1969 valedictorian, Mills College

8.

The World's Survival Choices

The need to make decisions about the survival of mankind is upon us right now, because the future is breaking in all over the place. But a growing number of us are refusing to participate in the making of these future-shaping decisions. We are tired. We have grown weary of the never-ending demand that we *do* something—right now—to ward off yet another disaster which is about to do us in.

We are victims of future shock!

Decision-Making and the Future

Future Shock is the title of a book by Alvin Toffler which appeared in 1970. Mr. Toffler (in a summary in *New York* magazine, July 27, 1970) argues that we are in shock because three powerful forces are simultaneously pushing at us and altering our psychological landscape. The three forces are:

1. *Acceleration*. This refers to the pace of change, the rate at which things, places, people, and other elements of our environment turn over. Acceleration affects the nature of human relationships especially. Knowing how temporary most new relationships will be, we subconsciously guard against letting them become too deep. We project only for the short-term, and increasingly our relationships show it. The effect of acceleration on decision-making, of course, is to demand that we make choices faster and faster.

2. *Novelty*. This is the need to cope with the non-routine, with strange situations perhaps daily. It is having not one but several new crises each day—not in world politics so much as in the once-routine daily activity. It is most prevalent in the largest cities, with their mix of peoples with conflicting values and their heavy reliance on technology to move people, messages, goods, and waste from one place to another. It is getting to work an hour late because your system of transportation malfunctioned, finding the elevators not working, the phone system fouled up, a demonstration featuring a nude young lady outside your building —and wondering what will happen next. It is all very tiring to body and spirit.

3. *Diversity*. This refers to the increased variety of choices available. Toffler suggests that, whereas the industrial era originally did bring much standardization and choicelessness, the trend today is in the other direction. He writes: "What is significant . . . is that part of the Super Industrial Revolution is an enormously powerful push, just now beginning, toward differentiation and diversity."

Toffler sees this trend confirmed by today's emphasis on individualized instruction, on ethnic independence if not separatism, on subcultures which come and go with the seasons, on the dazzling array of choices in the consumer marketplace.

He argues further that "Diversity, like novelty, is a mixed blessing. It too collides frontally with the accelerative pressures that demand speed in decision-making. Every psychological experiment on this subject indicates that decisions slow down as the number of options increases. Reaction time is longer when you have to choose between 100 alternative striped ties instead of 25 . . . "

It is logical that diversity should slow up the decision-making process, since more data must be taken in, sorted, and evaluated. It is the same, Toffler reminds us, not only "in the executive suite of General Electric or in the corridors of City Hall, but in the private adaptive choices made by all of us every day as we attempt to cope with our environment. . . . And it is precisely at our ability to make rational decisions that future shock strikes."

If Toffler is correct, then our making of choices in the future and about the future will not get any easier. But the truth is, despite the frightful face which the future seems more and more to be showing us, *we still do have choices—* and also, still, the ability to choose.

It is, indeed, one proof of God's grace that we have options. To be without choices, with no way to turn, is to have God's grace removed. Conversely, the fact that God still permits us to perceive and to choose among alternatives is a gift of his grace that we dare never take for granted.

Peace, People, and Pollution

What then are some of the choices before us, before all of mankind, in the years just ahead?—And it is no over-statement to term them *survival* choices. To my mind, they boil down to three: (1) the decision about how to resolve differences between nations or conflicting groups within nations; (2) the decision about how many people this planet can accommodate; (3) the decision about our relationship to the environment.

The first might be called the peace question. But that could be misleading, since "peace" sometimes suggests an absence of conflict. And to make that our goal is simply foolish. There just will not be a time when human beings live without conflict, nor should there be. For conflict is necessary to the unfolding of history, implicit in change, and potentially creative at least as much as it is destructive.

What we can hope for is a time when conflicts are not resolved by *violent* means. That implies, certainly, that we work and pray for the permanent retirement of military means for the settling of disputes among nations.

We have, at least for the better part of three decades, re-frained from using nuclear force to settle disputes. It is theoretically just as possible, in mutual self-interest, to refrain from taking up other kinds of arms against our fellowmen.

I do not believe we will ever completely do away with

murder, with the occasional destruction of one or more individuals by another. But we have at least established that such aberrations are *crimes*. We have yet to agree as a human community that war is just as much a crime. The fact that my nation's government may sanction an organized campaign of killing does not, in fact, make it any less homicidal, any less criminal.

It has often been observed that wars will cease when the young refuse to fight them and the old who plot and program the wars will have to do battle themselves, with their own bodies on the line. In places like North America, Western Europe, and Japan, we may be developing a generation of young people who, in growing numbers, simply refuse to participate in making war. If the young of the world have more in common with each other than with the earlier generations of their own countries and cultures, can we begin to hope?

The chief threat to the world's peace in the years ahead will not be the communism/capitalism tension, but the widening gap between rich nations and poor. It is now no longer a struggle between East and West, but between North and South: the generally affluent peoples of the northern hemisphere against the largely impoverished peoples of the southern hemisphere.

To quote again the overworked but most dramatic statistic: every inhabitant of the United States consumes about eight times the world's average in the resources of this planet. Even more disturbing: in one lifetime I will use up about 50 times as much of the consumables of Spaceship Earth as will one peasant in India.

Liberation, it has been said, is the new name for peace. Liberation of the world's South will require substantial concessions on the part of the world's North—in terms of sacrificing economic advantage, changing international trade agreements, and accepting some kind of world tax system which redistributes a part of the wealth. Justice, brotherhood, and peace—the absence of violent conflict—will require it.

The decisions about population are, if anything, more complex than those relating to war and world justice. For one thing, a lot of us have to unlearn some values that are profoundly held. We can all agree that, even in the name of country and flag, killing people isn't such a great idea. But we can hardly expect having babies to acquire war's bad image. Indeed, for many of the world's people, having babies is the one creative activity, the one freedom of self-expression, which has not been taken away.

Few persons will deny that world population growth needs to be checked. I know of no one who thinks the limited resources of the earth can be stretched to sustain population of ever-expanding size. The task is not to make motherhood unpopular, but to make *indiscriminate* motherhood unpopular.

I sense that it's already beginning to happen in the United States. Because of the propaganda campaign of recent years, and the increased sensitivity we all have to the possibility of overpopulation, some of my friends are embarrassed about having more than two or three children. Those of us from large families are assured that the social disapproval will not be made retroactive, but there is surely developing an attitude which suggests it is irresponsible to have a lot of babies.

The slogan of an organization called Zero Population Growth, "Stop at Two," has caught on with a large number of America's young people. Others propose that couples acquire their self-replacing pair by procreating one and adopting one. Some few, like the young lady quoted at the head of this chapter, believe they must, in the name of social responsibility, add *no* new persons to the world's population.

Most nations of the world have, by tax systems or other inducements, encouraged the growth of population through high birth rate. We can choose, if we will, to discard such pro-natalist policies. Indeed, such proposals are now being considered by law-making bodies in many parts of the world. Income tax credits for dependents in the United States, for example, could extend only to the first two children instead of continuing without limit.

The population question is more difficult among the poor, who still make up a majority of the earth's inhabitants, than among middle-class people of North America and Western Europe. We have already mentioned the strong psychological need to produce children, which seems especially pronounced among those who have been permitted little else. But there is another factor in cultures where security for the old lies in having children who will take care of you. And where infant and child mortality have been traditionally high, you need to give birth to many children to be sure there will be some surviving for your old-age security.

Even among those nations with highly developed systems of social security, the limitation of family size and stabilization of population will have consequences we are only now beginning to fathom. The pressure for population stabilization is surely leading to:

- greater freedom for men and women to choose how they will control their fertility, including removal of most abortion restrictions, and freer access to voluntary sterilization for both men and women

- development and greater acceptance of alternative roles for women, with the concomitant redefinition of what it means to be a male as well

- some change in the meaning of human sexuality, divorcing it more and more from the purely procreative.

The third big decision concerning our future—the relationship to our environment—is really inseparable from the population issue. Pollution is a problem because there are too many people. Or, as someone has remarked, people are not only the worst polluters, they are also the greatest pollutant.

But even if we should stabilize our population, the pollution battle would be far from won. One way of measuring the extent of the problem is by looking to what once was the gauge of national health: the Gross National Product. The fact is that a zooming GNP, as far as man's harmonious relationship to nature is concerned, leads not to health but to suicide. As an oilman said recently, "You want gas in the car? Okay, you get oil on the beach." [1]

And it's really just about that simple. Continuous growth in consumption becomes self-destructive, like the growth that is cancer. But how can you convince Americans, of all people? More than any other society in history, ours has been built on the principle that growth in the economy is essential. "Grow or die" has been a slogan central to the American way of life.

But we are going to hear more, much more, from other kinds of voices. Voices like that of John Fischer:

> Our prime national goal, I am now convinced, should be to reach Zero Growth Rate as soon as possible. Zero growth in people, in GNP, and in our consumption of everything. That is the only hope of attaining a stable ecology: that is, of halting the deterioration of the environment on which our lives depend. [2]

Some economists seem to hope that if economic growth through increased population ends, we will still have growth through increased per capita consumption. That won't do. We need to develop a life style of restraint. That means a lowered living standard. I don't know if Americans are capable of voting such restraints on their consumption. But all kinds of nations have accepted austerity under threat of war. And I have the strong belief that lowered living standard is preferable to extinction through ecological destruction.

I suppose, if it comes to that, we can have the cynical satisfaction that at least we wrecked the place for the most

American of reasons: to make a buck. It really *has* come down, you see, to money or trees.

Let me close this section with the reminder that pollution of our physical environment is not the only kind. There is a pollution of the spirit which has been with us humans from the beginning. It's often called sin. It's behind all our other problems, including destruction of the ecology by which we survive.

The following observation about it brings this section full circle, back to the first of our three arenas of future-shaping decision:

> . . . The spiritual environment . . . is heavily polluted, more so than the external one has ever been, and it now threatens us with extinction. The spiritual environment is befouled with hatred, fear, jealousy, brutality, and rapacity: with the craving for domination and the shortsighted narrow national egotism and expansionism that could make our globe uninhabitable. . . .
>
> When mankind's spiritual environment is considered from a distance, it looks much the same as Lake Erie looks now at close range—thoroughly polluted. We find, for example, a great nation that started its existence by demanding equal rights for everyone occupied in spending its means to build monstrous machines and organizations for the purpose of killing. . . . We find that same great technically developed nation showering millions of tons of napalm and herbicides on its less well-developed opponent, and find it justifying the slaughter of its own sons by showing that ten times as many "enemy" are being killed. . . .
>
> The cleansing of our spiritual environment is surely mankind's most compelling problem.[3]

Is There Any Hope?

Now, if I may add two concluding thoughts, I'll step out of the way and let you get on with your making of choices.

One is that none of the problems we have discussed can ever be finally disposed of. Problems do not have solutions, after all—only resolutions into the next set of problems. Thus, some of today's major problems have emerged from what we believed were solutions to yesterday's. We can hope, though, that the new set of problems will represent an advance of some sort over the situation posed by the preceding set.

The second closing thought is that there is hope. And that's not just a word to give the book a happy ending. It's a word from the gospel. We, the human beings whom God has placed here to manage this world, are still in control. We can change things through the choices we make.

Just as all our problems are the result of past choices made by men, including the one attributed to Adam and Eve in the Garden, so we can attack those problems—shift them to a new set at least—by the choices we make now. The damage done by human choice can be undone by human choice. And God is with us as we make those choices. He continues to care about his people, his creation, his universe.

But the choices are ours to make. There is no escaping that. That is what makes us free and human beings, under God—the capacity to make choices. He chose us for this.

NOTES

Chapter 1

1. From *Gideon* by Paddy Chayefsky. Copyright © 1961, 1962 by Carnegie Productions, Inc. Reprinted by permission of Random House, Inc.

2. "Will Judaism Survive the Seventies?" by Murray Saltzman. *Christian Century,* March 4, 1970, p. 264.

3. Quoted by Saltzman, *op. cit.*

Chapter 2

1. "The Responsibility of the Church for Society" by H. Richard Niebuhr in *The Gospel, the Church and the World,* ed. by K. S. Latourette (New York: Harper and Brothers, 1946), p. 130.

Chapter 3

1. *A Theological Word Book of the Bible,* ed. by Alan Richardson. Article on "Choose" by Norman H. Snaith. Copyright © 1955. The Macmillan Co. Reprinted by permission.

2. *The Great Divorce* by C. S. Lewis. (New York: Macmillan Paperbacks, 1946), p. 72.

3. "Religion and Prejudice" by Gregory Baum. *The Ecumenist,* July-August, 1968, pp. 167-171. Reprinted by permission.

Chapter 4

1. Quoted in "How America Lives with Death" by Kenneth L. Woodward. *Newsweek,* April 6, 1970, p. 89.

Chapter 6

1. *Church Politics* by Keith Bridston. (Cleveland: World Publishing, 1970), p. 163.

2. *Event* magazine, April 1970, p. 8.

125

3. Full statement is available from Office of the President, Lutheran Church in America, 231 Madison Ave., New York, N.Y. 10016.

4. *The Church for Others,* World Council of Churches (Department on Studies in Evangelism), Geneva, 1967, p. 78.

5. *Resistance, Rebellion, and Death* by Albert Camus, p. 71. Copyright © 1961. Alfred A. Knopf, Inc. Reprinted by permission.

6. *Commentary* magazine, April 1970, p. 37.

7. In an unpublished paper, "What Is the Responsibility of the Churches in Social Change?", available from Rev. Dean M. Kelley, 475 Riverside Drive, New York, N.Y. 10027.

Chapter 7

1. Quoted in "Song My—and the Myth of American Innocence" by Harold R. Fray Jr. *Tempo,* March 15, 1970.

2. *Ibid.*

3. *Ibid.*

4. Quoted in *Time-Life Library of America: the Old South,* Oliver E. Allen, ed. New York, 1968, p. 56.

5. Quoted in *Time-Life Library of America: the U.S. Overseas,* Oliver E. Allen, ed. New York, 1969, p. 27.

6. *Ibid.*

7. *Op. cit.,* p. 28.

8. *Ibid.*

9. *Op. cit.,* p. 38.

10. *Americans Betrayed* by M. Grodzins. (University of Chicago Press, 1969), p. 2.

11. *Op. cit.,* p. 283.

12. *New York Times* "The Week in Review," May 10, 1970. © 1970 by the New York Times Company. Reprinted by permission.

13. In an address to the U.S. Conference for the World Council of Churches, Buck Hill Falls, Pa., May 1, 1970.

14. Quoted in *Christianity and Crisis,* Jan. 8, 1968.

15. *Trans-Action,* March 1970, p. 40.

Chapter 8

1. Attributed to Bill Hopkins, an oil lobbyist in Alaska, and quoted in *Harper's,* May 1970, p. 102.

2. *Harper's,* April 1970, p. 20.

3. "The Third Environment" by Albert Szent-Gjorgi, *Saturday Review,* May 2, 1970. Copyright 1970 Saturday Review Inc. Reprinted by permission.

Charles P. Lutz was born "near the bottom of the depression, into an open-country Lutheran parsonage in southern Minnesota." After 12 years of public school in several Iowa small towns, he attended Wartburg College in Iowa and the Evangelical Lutheran Seminary in Columbus, Ohio. He and his wife Hertha "chose, more or less, to have three children," whose names are Timothy, Gretchen, and Nathan. Lutz chose not to receive ordination following seminary graduation, though he has worked professionally for church institutions ever since. For 10 years he edited Lutheran youth periodicals, including the monthly magazine *One*. The next three years he directed the Center for Urban Encounter, an ecumenical program of lay training in social change for Minnesota's Twin Cities area. From the summer of 1969 until the spring of 1971, he served the United States office of the World Council of Churches. In May 1971 he joined the Lutheran Council in the USA to coordinate a new service related to the choices all young men in America must face. He is the director of Lutheran Selective Service Information.